FUTURE
English for Results

4

WORKBOOK

Angela Blackwell
Therese Naber

Series Consultants
Beatriz B. Díaz
Ronna Magy
Federico Salas-Isnardi

PEARSON
Longman

Future 4
English for Results
Workbook

Pearson Education, 10 Bank Street, White Plains, NY 10606

Staff credits: The people who made up the *Future 4 Workbook* team, representing editorial, production, design, and manufacturing, are Peter Benson, Elizabeth Carlson, Aerin Csigay, Dave Dickey, Nancy Flaggman, Irene Frankel, Michael Kemper, Rebecca Ortman, Liza Pleva, Barbara Sabella, and Loretta Steeves.

Cover design: Rhea Banker
Cover photo: Kathy Lamm/Getty Images
Text design: Barbara Sabella
Text composition: Rainbow Graphics
Text font: 13 pt Minion

Illustration credits: Steve Attoe: pp. 70, 91; Laurie Conley: pp. 31, 143; Scott Fray: p. 63; Stephen Hutchings: pp. 71, 95; André Labrie: pp. 79, 107; Steve Schulman: pp. 27, 47, 85, 123; Gary Torrisi: pp. 59, 124, 131; Meryl Treatner: pp. 2, 51, 102; Anna Veltfort pp. 30, 111
Photo credits: p. 4 Jupiterimages/Brand X /Alamy; p. 11 Corbis Super RF/Alamy; p. 12 Shutterstock; p. 19 Shutterstock; p. 20 Jupiterimages; p. 32 Photo courtesy Bay Area Gardeners' Foundation; p. 34 Shutterstock; p. 35 David Hiller/Getty Images; p. 44 (top left) Shutterstock, (middle right) Shutterstock, (bottom left) Shutterstock, (bottom right) Stockbyte/Alamy; p. 50 Hero Images/Getty Images; p. 52 Doug Webb/Alamy; p. 54 Stockbyte Platinum/Getty Images; p. 55 Jupiterimages/Creatas/Alamy; p. 65 Roger McClean/iStockphoto.com; p. 68 Shutterstock; p. 75 (left) Shutterstock, (right) Shutterstock; p. 77 Shutterstock; p. 80 Shutterstock; p. 86 Shutterstock; p. 92 Shutterstock; p. 106 Kayte Deioma/PhotoEdit; p. 112 Corbis Premium RF/Alamy; p. 128 Ron Chapple/Getty Images; p. 135 Michelle D. Bridwell/ PhotoEdit; p. 136 Shutterstock; p. 138 Shutterstock.

ISBN-13: 978-0-13-199160-6
ISBN-10: 0-13-199160-4

Printed in the United States of America
13   16

Contents

To the Teacher iv

To the Student v

UNIT 1   Catching Up 2

UNIT 2   Tell Me about Yourself.................................. 14

UNIT 3   Community Life... 26

UNIT 4   On the Job.. 38

UNIT 5   Safe and Sound.. 50

UNIT 6   Moving In 62

UNIT 7   Behind the Wheel....................................... 74

UNIT 8   How Are You Feeling?.................................. 86

UNIT 9   Partners in Education.................................. 98

UNIT 10   Safety First.. 110

UNIT 11   Know the Law!.. 122

UNIT 12   Saving and Spending 134

Answer Key 146

The *Future 4 Workbook* has 12-page units to complement what students have learned in the Student Book. Each workbook unit follows the lesson order of the Student Book and provides supplemental practice in grammar, life skills, reading, writing, and vocabulary. Students can complete the exercises outside the classroom as homework or during class time to extend instruction.

UNIT STRUCTURE

Grammar

Grammar exercises include sentence completion, sentence writing, sentence scrambles, matching, and multiple choice. Exercises progress from very controlled to open and provide ample written practice with the target structure. Exercises are contextualized, recycling themes and vocabulary from the unit, so that grammar practice is authentic and meaningful.

Life Skills

Practice focuses on functional language, practical skills, and authentic printed materials such as apartment leases and income tax forms. Each Life Skill lesson also includes either a Dictionary Skill or Study Skill exercise. Designed to help students get the most from their dictionaries, Dictionary Skill exercises feature excerpts from the *Longman Dictionary of American English*. Study Skill exercises build students' abilities to interpret charts and graphs.

Reading

Each reading page includes a new, high-interest, informative article related to the theme of the Student Book unit. The structures and vocabulary in the texts are controlled so students can be successful readers. Reading Skills presented in the Student Book, such as finding the main idea, identifying the topic, and scanning for information, are reviewed and practiced through pre-reading or comprehension

tasks. As we know, the meaning of unknown words can sometimes be figured out from the context, and students need instruction and practice with this skill. Therefore, Word Work exercises that follow the reading selections direct students to use context clues to get the meaning of boldface words.

Writing

The writing page focuses on revising and editing. The lesson begins with a paragraph that a student might have written in response to the writing assignment in the Student Book. Students revise and edit the paragraph according to the writing tip presented in the Student Book. For example, students complete a paragraph by inserting sentences in chronological order or delete unnecessary information from a paragraph. The lesson concludes with an error-correction exercise in which students read a short paragraph and correct grammatical errors.

Vocabulary

Each unit in the Workbook culminates with a vocabulary lesson that reviews and expands on the vocabulary presented in the Student Book. Each vocabulary lesson includes a learning strategy tip, such as using visuals to help remember new words. These strategies support persistence by giving students ideas for continued learning outside the classroom and can be used with any new words students encounter.

ANSWER KEY

Answers to all exercises are found in the back of the Workbook.

ORIENTATION

Before the students use the Workbook for the first time, direct them to the *To the Student* material. Go through the questions with the class so students can get the most out of the Workbook.

To the Student

LEARN ABOUT YOUR BOOK

A PAIRS. Look at Unit 1. Write the subject of each lesson on the line. Use words from the box. Some words will be used more than once.

> grammar   life skills and study skills   reading   vocabulary   writing

Lesson 1 & 2: _____   Lesson 7 & 8: _____

Lesson 3: _____   Lessons 9: _____

Lesson 4 & 5: _____   Review & Expand: _____

Lessons 6: _____

B PAIRS. Look at Unit 1. Find a page where you can find the following information or activities. Write the page number on the line.

1. advice to help you become a better reader _____

2. practice reading and understanding different kinds of graphs _____

3. advice to help you improve your writing skills _____

4. advice to help you learn new vocabulary _____

C PAIRS. Look at page 29. What skill is practiced in Exercise A?

_____

D PAIRS. Look at page 146. Answer the questions.

1. What information is on this page? _____

2. Find *Answers will vary, but could include.* What does *Answers will vary* mean?

_____

A Complete the conversation between Alex and Rosa. Underline the correct words.

Alex: Excuse me. <u>**Does the 52 stop**</u> / **Is the 52 stopping** here?

Rosa: Yes, **I wait** / **I'm waiting** for the 52. Hey . . . Alex! **Do you remember** / **Are you remembering** me?

Alex: Rosa! Long time no see! How are you?

Rosa: I'm fine. But what **do you do** / **are you doing** here?

Alex: I work right across the street: over at Tito's.

Rosa: Really? That's funny. **I take** / **I'm taking** this bus every day, but **I never see** / **I'm never seeing** you.

Alex: Oh, **I don't usually take** / **I'm not usually taking** the bus. I usually drive to work. **I ride** / **I'm riding** the bus today because my wife **uses** / **is using** the car.

Rosa: Oh, I see.

Alex: What about you? What **do you do** / **are you doing** these days?

Rosa: Well, **I take** / **I'm taking** classes at the community center. **I want** / **I'm wanting** to get my GED.

Alex: That's great! Good for you!

B Complete the conversations. Use the simple present or the present continuous.

1. **A:** Good to see you, Phong! What ___are you doing___ these days?
   (you / do)

   B: I _____ to school. I _____ business.
   (go) **(study)**

   A: That's great! _____ it?
   (you / like)

   B: Yes . . . but it's a lot of work!

2. **A:** Hi Tomas! What _____ here?
   (you / do)

   B: I _____ for my girlfriend. She _____ me a ride to
   (wait) **(give)**
   school today.

3. **A:** What _____ in your free time?
   (you / do)

   B: I _____ any free time! I _____ two jobs right now.
   (not have) **(work)**

   A: Oh, my. You must be tired at the end of the day.

4. **A:** Guess what! I _____ a class at City College!
   (take)

   B: That's interesting. What _____?
   (you / studying)

   A: Nursing. I _____ to work in a hospital.
   (want)

C Complete the questions. Use *do* or *are*.

1. What time __do__ you get up on weekdays?

2. _____ you take a bus or a train every day?

3. _____ you work every day?

4. _____ you working this week?

5. How _____ you spend your free time?

6. How many hours a day _____ you usually speak English?

7. _____ you taking a morning class this semester?

8. _____ you planning to take a vacation this month?

BEFORE YOU READ

Skim the article. Underline the title and the section headings. Then answer the question.

What is the article about? _____

READ

Read the article. Circle the names of two people who believe that the American dream is still alive.

Questioning the American Dream

Every year, thousands of hopeful newcomers come to the United States in search of a better life. They believe that with hard work and determination they will succeed and guarantee a better future for their children. They believe in the American dream: that anybody can achieve a goal if he or she works hard enough.

TOUGH TIMES

However, the American dream is more **elusive** than it once was. Statistics show that it is harder now than it ever was before for people to move from one economic class to the next. More Americans worry about having enough money to take care of their family, own their own home, educate their children, and enjoy their **retirement**.

Last month, we asked readers the question, "Is the American dream still alive?" Here are some of the replies.

STILL ALIVE

Barbara Monteza, from Michigan, says: "The American dream is still alive! My father came here from El Salvador with nothing. His first job in the U.S. was as a janitor. After five years, he was able to start his own company. That's the best example of the American dream that I know."

NOT FOR EVERYONE

Reader Paul Connors disagrees: "The American dream is certainly not alive for everyone. Poor people in the U.S. are struggling to **get by**. They work hard and have nothing left over." Yvette Weiss, writing from Des Moines, adds that success nowadays is more about contacts. "You have to be in the right place at the right time. It's who you know, not what you do."

FREEDOM TO DREAM

Many readers insisted that the American dream is not about **material success**. Brian Miller of California writes, "The American dream is the freedom to dream of possibilities. You have to be able to dream before you can begin to make your dream into a reality. In that sense, the American dream is still very much alive."

CHECK YOUR UNDERSTANDING

A **Read the article again. Then read the statements. Circle *True* or *False*.**

1. People who come to the U.S. believe in the American dream.   **True**   **False**

2. The American dream is the belief that you can succeed if you work hard.   **True**   **False**

3. It is easier for people to succeed in the U.S. now than it was before.   **True**   **False**

4. Barbara Monteza's father became successful in the U.S.   **True**   **False**

5. Paul Connors and Yvette Weiss believe that it is easy to achieve the American dream.   **True**   **False**

6. Brian Miller believes that the American dream is not about money.   **True**   **False**

B **MAKE IT PERSONAL. What do you think? Is the American dream alive?**

_____

_____

C **WORD WORK. Find the boldface words in the article. Complete the sentences.**

1. If something is **elusive** it is _____.

   a. popular

   b. a reality

   c. hard to achieve

2. Your **retirement** is _____.

   a. money that you get for doing work

   b. the time when you stop working

   c. a place where older people live

3. When you can't **get by**, you can't _____.

   a. earn enough money to live on

   b. find a good job

   c. enter the U.S.

4. If you enjoy **material success**, you have _____.

   a. a lot of money

   b. good contacts

   c. a dream for the future

A Look at Maria's schedule for the week. Answer the questions with complete sentences. Use the present continuous or *going to*.

Monday **21**	9:00 – 12:00 computer class 3:00 meet with advisor
Tuesday **22**	1:00 – 9:00 work
Wednesday **23**	9:00 – 12:00 accounting class 1:00 – 9:00 work
Thursday **24**	10:00 meet Carlos at library 1:00 – 9:00 work

Friday **25**	9:00 – 12:00 study for test! 1:00 – 9:00 work
Saturday **26**	11:00 – 7:00 work 7:30 dinner with José
Sunday **27**	10 – 12 attend job fair 5:00 – 9:00 babysit for Diana

1. What is Maria doing at 3:00 P.M. on Monday? _____ *She's meeting with an advisor.* _____

2. What is she going to do on Tuesday? _____

3. What class is she taking on Wednesday morning? _____

4. Where is she meeting Carlos on Thursday? _____

5. What time is Maria going to work on Thursday? _____

6. What is she going to do on Friday morning? _____

7. What hours is she working on Saturday? _____

8. What is she going to do on Sunday morning? _____

B Complete the conversations. Use the future. Use contractions if possible.

1. **A:** Is that a wedding ring?

   B: Yes, it is! Tomasz and I _____are getting_____ married!
   (**get, present continuous**)

   A: That's great news. Where _____ the wedding?
   (**you / be going to / have**)

   B: We _____ it here. His parents _____ from Poland.
   (**have, present continuous**)   (**be going to / come**)

   A: Well, that's great! Congratulations! I'm sure you _____ very happy.
   (**will / be**)

2. **A:** Our class _____ a picnic next week. Can you come?
   (**have, present continuous**)

   B: I hope so. When is it?

   A: Right after class on Thursday. We _____ to the park.
   (**be going to / go**)

   B: That sounds good. I _____ something.
   (**will / bring**)

C Complete the conversation. Underline the correct words.

A: Are you going somewhere?

B: Yes. There's a job fair downtown, and (1.) **I'm going to go** / **I'll go**.

A: Really? Why?

B: Well, I'm looking for a job. So (2.) **I'm going to do** / **I'm doing** some research.

A: What about school? If you get a job, you won't have time to study.

B: Well, if I get a job, I guess (3.) **I'm going to study** / **I'll study** part time. Take a look at this.

A: What's that?

B: My résumé. (4.) **I'm going to show** / **I'll show** it to people. Maybe (5.) **I'm going to get** /

   I'll get an interview.

A: Good idea. How long (6.) **are you going to stay** / **will you stay**?

B: Only until noon. I have to go to a class after that.

A: Maybe (7.) **I'm going to go** / **I'll go** with you.

B: Sure, come on! (8.) **I'm going to wait** / **I'll wait** for you.

LIFE SKILLS

A Read the college course enrollment form. How many courses is the student enrolling in? _____

Newby College

NEWBY COLLEGE
2310 WILLOW AVENUE
MADISON, CA 94321

123-67-0000   04   29   85

Social Security Number   Birthdate: Month   Day   Year

POON   ESTHER   M

Last Name   First Name   Middle Initial

Gender: M ☐   F ☑

2376   53rd Ave   Apt. 4

Address: Number   Street   Apartment

Madison   CA   94322

City   State   Zip Code

E-mail Address: estherp342@future.net

Phone Number:

Day   651-555-9075   Evening   651-555-0992

Citizenship:

U.S. Citizen ☐   Green Card Holder ☑   Other ☐ _____

Course Number	Course Title	Units	Fee
4539	Management in the Hotel Industry	2	130
6290	Accounting Principles	2	150

Type of Payment (check one):   Total Payment: _____ 280

☑ Check

☐ Money Order

Signature   *Esther Poon*   Date   August 3, 2010

Submit to Office of Admissions, Room 403, Humanities Building

OR Fax to 651-555-8003 OR Enroll Online at Newbycollege/enroll.com

---

B **Read the enrollment form again. Answer the questions.**

1. What school is this application form for? _____

2. Who is applying to the school? _____

3. What courses is the student applying for? _____

4. What personal information does the student give? _____

5. What does the student have to submit with the application? _____

6. How can the student send in the application? _____

C **MAKE IT PERSONAL. What kinds of school courses or programs have you enrolled in?**

_____

_____

STUDY SKILL: Use a bar graph

Look at the bar graph. Answer the questions.

1. What are the median weekly earnings of a worker with an associate's degree? _____

2. What are the median weekly earnings of a worker without a high school diploma? _____

3. How much more does a worker with a bachelor's degree earn per week than a worker with only a high school diploma? _____

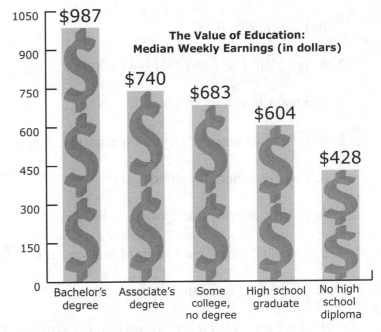

The Value of Education:
Median Weekly Earnings (in dollars)

$987 — Bachelor's degree
$740 — Associate's degree
$683 — Some college, no degree
$604 — High school graduate
$428 — No high school diploma

Source: *Bureau of Labor Statistics*

A **Complete the paragraph. Use the simple past.**

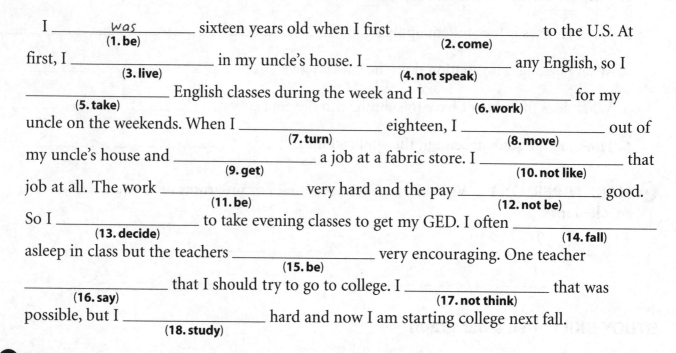

I _____was_____ sixteen years old when I first _____ to the U.S. At
      (1. be)   **(2. come)**
first, I _____ in my uncle's house. I _____ any English, so I
         (3. live)   **(4. not speak)**
_____ English classes during the week and I _____ for my
   (5. take)   **(6. work)**
uncle on the weekends. When I _____ eighteen, I _____ out of
                               (7. turn)   **(8. move)**
my uncle's house and _____ a job at a fabric store. I _____ that
                      (9. get)   **(10. not like)**
job at all. The work _____ very hard and the pay _____ good.
                      (11. be)   **(12. not be)**
So I _____ to take evening classes to get my GED. I often _____
     (13. decide)   **(14. fall)**
asleep in class but the teachers _____ very encouraging. One teacher
                                  (15. be)
_____ that I should try to go to college. I _____ that was
   (16. say)   **(17. not think)**
possible, but I _____ hard and now I am starting college next fall.
                 (18. study)

B **Complete the conversations. Unscramble the sentences. Make questions.**

1. **A:** (come / did / the / U.S. / you / to / when) _____ When did you come to the U.S.? _____

   B: Five years ago.

2. **A:** (go / did / to / you / school / where) _____

   B: I went to school in Ukraine.

3. **A:** (at / did / how / Telemax / work / you / long) _____

   B: I worked there for three years.

4. **A:** (kind / did / of / do / work / what / you) _____

   B: I worked in the mail room. I sent out and received letters and packages.

5. **A:** (did / job / like / that / you) _____

   B: Yes, I did. But I'd like to work in the computer industry.

C Complete the conversation about Selma's life in Brazil. Use the simple past.

Chris: How _____was_____ your life in Brazil?
(**1. be**)

Selma: Oh, it _____ very different. We
(**2. be**)

_____ in Rio de Janeiro, so the
(**3. live**)

weather _____ warm.
(**4. be**)

Chris: Where _____?
(**5. you, live**)

Selma: We _____ a house. It
(**6. own**)

_____ really small!
(**7. be**)

There _____ eight people in the family, so it was crowded!
(**8. be**)

Chris: _____ in Rio?
(**9. you, work**)

Selma: No. I _____ out to work. I _____ home.
(**10. not go**)   (**11. stay**)

I _____ care of my children and my sisters' children.
(**12. take**)

Chris: What _____ every day?
(**13. you, do**)

Selma: Well, I _____ the house. I _____ groceries at the
(**14. clean**)   (**15. buy**)

market and I _____ a big meal every day.
(**16. make**)

Chris: _____ a car?
(**17. you, have**)

Selma: No. I _____ everywhere on the bus.
(**18. go**)

D Read about Selma's life in the U.S. Then look at the conversation in Exercise C again. On notepaper, write sentences about how Selma's life has changed since she left Brazil. Use *used to* and *didn't use to*.

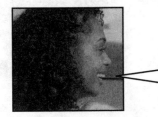

Now I live in Portland, Oregon. It's often rainy and cold here! I work in a hotel, and I live in an apartment, not a house. I have a car, and I drive to work and to the store. I'm very busy, so I don't have time to cook: I eat a lot of fast food!

Selma used to live in Rio, but now she lives in Portland.

Ⓐ Complete the paragraph about a role model. Use the sentences in the box.

Sometimes he studied until two in the morning.
He started taking English classes in 1999.
In 2005, he started working in a local hospital.
He came to the U.S. from Haiti in 1998.

Writing Tip

When you write a biographical paragraph, put information about the person's life in chronological (time) order.

My Uncle Alfonse is my role model. I have learned a lot from him. Uncle Alfonse was a medical technician in Haiti. (1.) _____ He came with his wife, Josette, and their three children. My uncle Alfonse worked as a dishwasher in a restaurant for several years. (2.) _____ Uncle Alfonse was determined to learn English and work as a medical technician here. He worked all day and then took classes in the evening. (3.) _____ _____ It took several years of hard work before his English was good enough for him to take the exams he needed to work as a medical technician in the U.S. (4.) _____ He loves his job. Now he works during the day and can finally relax with his family in the evening.

Ⓑ Read the paragraph. Correct four more mistakes.

My role model is my husband's grandmother. Grandma Li ~~come~~ *came* to the U.S. from China and raise five children here. She didn't speak English, but she valued education and make sure all the children worked hard in school. No one in the family had gone to college before, but all five of her children are college graduates. Now her children are grown and Grandma Li finally have time to study English. She take classes and volunteers at an elementary school.

A Read about Ali. Then continue the paragraph. Use the expressions in the box and your own ideas.

Ali wanted to get ahead, so he set a goal for himself: to complete his GED. He enrolled in classes at a community college. After two years, he managed to fulfill his dream.

> **Learning Strategy:**
> Write a Story
>
> Write a story using new vocabulary words. By putting the vocabulary into a story, you give the words context and make them more memorable.

attend a job search workshop	~~do research~~	get a job
have an interview	send in an application	

Ali wanted a new job, so he started to do research. _____

_____

_____

B Complete the sentences. Use the words in the box.

ambitious	dependable	~~determined~~	disciplined
goal-oriented	hardworking	successful	

1. Hussein has a lot of determination. He's _____determined_____.

2. I hope that Tatiana's business is a success. I hope that she is _____.

3. My brother has a lot of ambition. He's _____.

4. Ho Jin works very hard. He's a _____ student.

5. You can depend on Miguel. He's _____.

6. If you are self-employed, you need a lot of discipline. You must be _____.

7. She sets goals and works toward them. She's _____.

Lessons 1 & 2: Grammar

 A **Complete the chart. Check (✓) if the verb can be followed by an infinitive or a gerund. Some verbs can be followed by both.**

	infinitive *to go*	gerund *going*		infinitive *to go*	gerund *going*
I wanted	✓		I need		
They like			You would like		
We decided			She enjoys		
Let's discuss			We prefer		
She started			They continued		
He recommended			He hopes		

B **Complete the conversation. Circle the correct words. If both answers are correct, circle both.**

Soo-Jin: How was your meeting at the job center today?

Luis: Good. We discussed to **set** / (**setting**) short-term and long-term goals. I'm going to finish **to work** / **working** on them tonight. But, I'm getting a little worried.

Soo-Jin: Why?

Luis: I'd like **to wait** / **waiting** for the right job, but I need **to make** / **making** money soon.

Soo-Jin: Maybe you should consider **to find** / **finding** a part-time job, and then you can continue **to look** / **looking** in your free time.

Luis: Maybe you're right. I'd really like **to find** / **finding** something in my field, though.

Soo-Jin: Maybe you can find something in your field. You won't know until you start **to look** / **looking**.

C Read the e-mail message. Find and correct five more mistakes with gerunds or infinitives.

From: Gail Park

To: Luis Costa

Subject: Possible job?

Hi Luis,

I don't know if you've begun ^to^ look for a job yet, but I heard about a part-time customer service rep position at Allied Electric. A friend of mine works there and told me about the position. I thought of you because you enjoy to work with people! I know you want finding a full-time position, but this might be a start. You could get some good experience and my friend said that if things go well, you could apply working more hours later. She thinks it's a good company and enjoys to work there. I think you should consider to send in your résumé.

Gail

D MAKE IT PERSONAL. Write four sentences on notepaper about your work goals and preferences. Use words in the chart or your own ideas.

I want	work	with people
I enjoy	use	long hours
I don't like	commute	in an office
I'd like	find	my degree
I hope	earn	a long distance to work
I prefer	look for	a full-time position
I decided	complete	more money

I prefer to work with people.

LIFE SKILLS

A Complete the résumé. Use the headings in the box.

> Achievements   Education   Objective
> Qualifications   Related Experience

Lorena Medina
1893 Juniper Road
Hayward, CA 94541
(510) 555-9367
lmedina@mymail.com

1. _____

To work as a manager in a restaurant or retail store

2. _____

* Experienced at managing store operations in a fast-paced environment
* Able to work as part of a team and lead others
* Skilled at giving excellent customer service
* Able to increase sales and achieve goals
* Proficient at reviewing sales figures and predicting future sales

3. _____

Store Manager   Managed and supervised 15 employees. Organized employee work
2007–Present   schedules. Hired and trained new employees. Kept accurate records of
Kim's Coffee   inventory. Responsible for ordering supplies and receiving shipments.
Palo Alto, CA

Sales Associate   Assisted customers and used cash register. Responsible for receiving
2002–2007   shipments and stocking shelves.
Kali Imports
Hayward, CA

4. _____

* Received "Super Seller" award in 2006 for increasing store sales by 25%
* Named "Manager of the Year" in 2007 and 2008

5. _____

B.S., Communications
Bay View College
San Francisco, CA

References available upon request.

B **Read the statements about Lorena. Circle *True* or *False*.**

1. Lorena wants a job as a sales associate.   **True**   **False**

2. She works at Kali Imports now.   **True**   **False**

3. She has experience as a store manager.   **True**   **False**

4. She supervised fifteen workers at Kim's Coffee.   **True**   **False**

5. She has worked at Kim's Coffee since 2002.   **True**   **False**

6. She has a college degree.   **True**   **False**

STUDY SKILL: Use a bar graph

Look at the bar graph. Answer the questions.

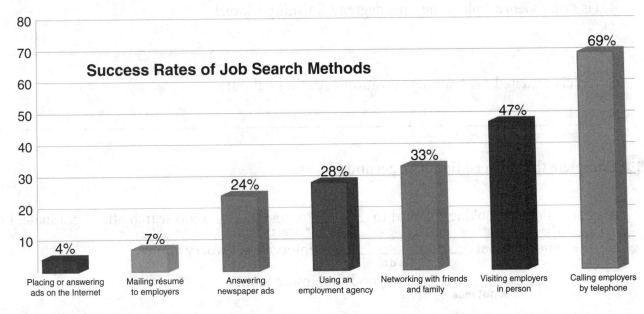

Source: *Monthly Labor Review.*

1. Which is the most successful job search method? _____

2. Which is the least successful? _____

3. Which search method has a 7 percent success rate? _____

4. What percentage of people got a job by answering newspaper ads? _____

5. What percentage of people got a job by networking with friends? _____

A Unscramble the sentences. One sentence is a question.

1. (I'm / applying for / interested / the sales job / in)

   I'm interested in applying for the sales job.

2. (capable / other employees / of / Linh / is / managing)

   _____

3. (looking / to / we're / forward / hiring / some new employees)

   _____

4. (is / on / Gebru / planning / his degree / finishing / soon)

   _____

5. (Alicia / excited / is / her new position / starting / about)

   _____

B Complete the conversation. Use gerunds.

Alex: I'm not looking forward to _____starting_____ a job search after I graduate. I'm
(1. start)

not good at _____ interviews. I worry about
(2. do)

_____ a good first impression.
(3. not make)

Carmen: Don't worry. We can plan on _____ before you start looking.
(4. practice)

Alex: Actually, I'm thinking about _____ for a job at the Grand Café.
(5. apply)

Carmen: Really? I didn't know you were interested in _____ in a restaurant.
(6. work)

Alex: Oh yes. I plan on _____ my own café some day.
(7. own)

Carmen: That's a good idea. You're good at _____.
(8. cook)

C Complete the conversation. Use the words in the box. Use gerunds.

> do   fix   have   quit   stay   use   ~~work~~

Ana: What's the matter?

Joel: Oh, I'm not happy with my job. I'm tired of (1.) _____working_____ long hours, but
I'm afraid of (2.) _____ and not finding something else.

Ana: It sounds like you have to choose between (3.) _____ and being
unhappy, or leaving and possibly finding a good new job.

Joel: Yes, you're right, but I don't know how to begin a job search.

Ana: Well, what are you interested in (4.) _____?

Joel: I'm not sure. I enjoy (5.) _____ computers, and I'm good at
(6.) _____ them.

Ana: Maybe you should look for a position repairing computers.

Joel: But I'm worried about not (7.) _____ a computer degree.

Ana: Well, maybe you don't need one. You should do some research and find out.

D Read about Jin-Sil. Write sentences about her job abilities and plans. Use
the words in parentheses and gerunds.

I want to work
with people. I can
supervise other
workers. I solve
problems well. I
want to go back to
school in the future.

Jin-Sil

1. (**interested in**) _Jin-Sil is interested in_
   working with people.

2. (**capable of**) _____
   _____

3. (**good at**) _____
   _____

4. (**plan on**) _____
   _____

READ

Read the article. Circle two forms of sexual harassment.

Sexual Harassment in the Workplace

Sabrina Mendes worked as the assistant manager at a large chain store. She was an excellent employee and had been with the company for seven years. When her manager decided to transfer to another store, Sabrina hoped to be promoted to his position.

However, at a job performance meeting, Sabrina's manager made it clear that he would only recommend Sabrina for the promotion if she went on a date with him. Sabrina told her manager she was not interested in dating him. As a result, the manager recommended a less qualified worker, who was promoted instead.

"This type of behavior is called quid pro quo sexual harassment," says legal advisor Marie Park. "When a job benefit is offered to an employee in exchange for **unwelcome** sexual advances, it's a form of sexual harassment."

Angry at how she had been treated, Sabrina explained what had happened to an upper-level supervisor. The supervisor

helped Sabrina file a complaint against her manager, and she eventually won her case.

Sexual harassment doesn't only involve getting a job or promotion and the harasser doesn't have to be a supervisor—he or she can be a manager in another department, a coworker, or even a client. According to Park, the most common form of sexual harassment occurs when behavior of a sexual nature leads to a **hostile** work environment. This behavior includes unwanted physical contact, sexual comments or jokes, displays of **offensive** materials such as pornography, and repeated invitations for dates after being rejected. The behavior makes the workplace so **intolerable** that it prevents an employee from doing his or her job.

"The important thing," says Park, "is for employees to know their rights if they experience this behavior at work. Sexual harassment is **illegal**. Keep a record of what happened and be ready to take your complaint to a higher level if necessary."

CHECK YOUR UNDERSTANDING

A Which of the following situations is an example of quid pro quo sexual harassment? Check (✓) the correct answer.

_____ a. A manager fires an employee after she rejects the manager's sexual advances.

_____ b. A coworker puts a pornographic picture on his office wall.

_____ c. A manager repeatedly asks an employee for a date even after he has been rejected.

_____ d. A manager offers an employee more hours if she goes on a date with him.

B According to the article, what are four examples of sexual harassment that can lead to a hostile work environment?

Reading Skill:
Using Details to Understand Important Ideas

Look for details to help you understand an author's ideas more completely.

1. _____

2. _____

3. _____

4. _____

C Read the article again. Read the statements. Circle *True* or *False*.

1. Sabrina believed that she was qualified for the manager position.   **True   False**

2. Sabrina decided to transfer to another store.   **True   False**

3. Sabrina's manager wanted to go on a date with her.   **True   False**

4. Sabrina made it clear she was not interested in dating her manager.   **True   False**

5. Sabrina's manager gave the promotion to another employee because the other employee had more experience.   **True   False**

6. Sabrina was a victim of quid pro quo sexual harassment.   **True   False**

7. Sabrina complained about her manager's behavior.   **True   False**

D WORD WORK. Find the boldface words in the article. Then match the words with the definitions. Write the letter on the line.

1. ____ **unwelcome**   a. not allowed by the law

2. ____ **hostile**   b. difficult to accept

3. ____ **offensive**   c. angry, unfriendly, or difficult

4. ____ **intolerable**   d. very impolite or insulting

5. ____ **illegal**   e. not wanted or needed

A Complete the conversation. Use the present perfect. Use contractions if possible.

Tin: How long ___have you worked___ at Allied Company?
(**1. you / work**)

Lee: I _____ here for five years. I _____ several different
(**2. work**)   (**3. have**)
positions.

Tin: What different jobs _____?
(**4. do**)

Lee: Well, I _____ in customer service, and I _____ two
(**5. work**)   (**6. supervise**)
other employees.

Tin: _____ any sales work?
(**7. you / ever / do**)

Lee: No, I _____ in sales. I don't think I'd be good at it!
(**8. not / work**)

B Complete the conversations. Choose the correct words.

1. **A:** I **never worked** / (**have never worked**) in sales. How about you?

   B: Yes, I **did** / **have**.

2. **A:** Ivan is my best employee. He **worked** / **has worked** here for almost ten years.

   B: Really? I thought he **started** / **has started** last year!

3. **A:** When **did you get** / **have you gotten** your current job?

   B: I **started** / **have started** in 2003.

4. **A:** How long **did you know** / **have you known** Fabio?

   B: A long time. We **met** / **have met** in 1999, and we **were** / **have been** friends ever since.

5. **A:** Leticia **got** / **has gotten** a promotion last week. She's a supervisor now.

   B: That's great! She **worked** / **has worked** here for a long time. She deserves it.

C **Complete the paragraph. Use the simple past or present perfect.**

I ____have lived____ in the U.S. since 2005. I _____ working as soon as
    (1. live)   **(2. start)**

I arrived. My first job _____ in a restaurant. I _____ as a
                          (3. be)   **(4. work)**

dishwasher. Then I _____ another position as a server. I
                         (5. get)

_____ English in the evening, and I _____ during the day.
   (6. study)   **(7. work)**

However, I _____ to find a better job. I _____ interested in
             (8. want)   **(9. be)**

working with children all my life. So, I _____ to go back to school. I
                                (10. decide)

_____ seven classes already and I hope to finish my degree next semester. I
  (11. take)

_____ A's and B's in every class so far. I _____ full time since
  (12. get)   **(13. not work)**

I started school, but I _____ as a teaching assistant for the past year. I love
                     (14. work)

the work and can't wait to finish my degree!

D **Look at Viktor's timeline. Write about his work experience. Write two
sentences using the simple past and two sentences using the present perfect.**

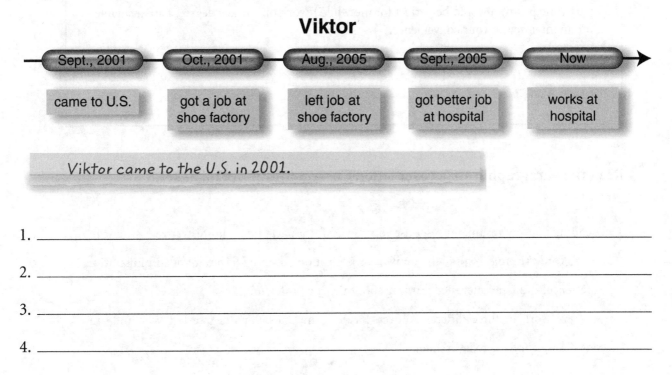

Viktor

Sept., 2001	Oct., 2001	Aug., 2005	Sept., 2005	Now
came to U.S.	got a job at shoe factory	left job at shoe factory	got better job at hospital	works at hospital

Viktor came to the U.S. in 2001.

1. _____

2. _____

3. _____

4. _____

A Read the résumé cover letter. Cross out three more unnecessary sentences in the letter.

> Dear Ms. Zhang,
>
> I am sending you my résumé in response to your online ad for a part-time administrative assistant at Miller and Planck Law Firm. ~~I have been looking for a job like this for several weeks now.~~ I am interested in the position because it fits well with my education, experience, and interests.
>
> I have a bachelor's degree in anthropology from Dell College, and I am starting the law program there next month. For the past two summers, I worked as an intern at Samuels and Carr Law here in Ann Arbor. My supervisor's name was Jim Matz, and I really enjoyed working for him. Through that experience, I learned about day-to-day operations at a law firm and utilized my strong organizational skills.
>
> I am familiar with the environmental law work that your firm does. I love the outdoors and enjoy hiking, camping, and canoeing. I plan on specializing in environmental law and would love to have the opportunity to learn more by working at Miller and Planck. A part-time position would be perfect for me while I work on my law degree. I am available for an interview at your convenience.
>
> Sincerely,
>
> *Guy Duval*

B Read the paragraph from a cover letter. Correct four more mistakes.

>   *am*
> I sending you my résumé in response to your ad for a part-time administrative assistant in today's *Daily Tribune*. I would like apply for the position because I have a lot of administrative experience, and I am interested learning about the law profession.
>
>   I have work in three different offices. I receive my bachelor's degree last year and am considering applying to law school.

A Complete the mind map. Use the words in the box. Write the words on the lines. Then add your own word for each preposition.

> afraid   believe   capable   concerned
> good   interested   skilled   worried

Learning Strategy:
Use Mind Maps

Make a mind map to organize vocabulary and help you to remember new words and expressions.

afraid (of)

(about)

(at)

(in)

B Complete the chart. Then complete the sentences. Use the words in the chart.

Verb	Noun	Noun (person)
develop	development	developer
know		X
require		X
	response	X
assist	assistance	
		applicant

1. One ___requirement___ for the position is a college degree.

2. Joe learned a lot at his first job. For example, it helped him _____ very strong communications skills.

3. The Job Center offers job search _____ to anyone who needs help.

4. The company is looking for someone with _____ of web design.

5. I sent in my résumé a month ago, but I've had no _____. I've heard nothing.

6. Felix is going to _____ for a job at the hospital.

A Complete the sentences. Use *about*, *at*, *in*, *of*, or *with*. More than one answer may be possible.

1. Ya-Wen is worried _____*about*_____ moving to a new neighborhood.

2. Pilar is frustrated _____ her poor English.

3. We'd like to move to a quieter neighborhood. We're tired _____ the noise.

4. I'm interested _____ finding out about after-school programs.

5. Are you pleased _____ your new apartment?

6. I was surprised _____ the number of apartments in the building.

7. My neighbor is often annoyed _____ the people who park in his driveway.

B Complete the conversation. Circle the correct words.

Hong: How do you like your new neighborhood?

Karine: Well, we've only been here a few weeks, but it's **interested /(interesting.)**

I'm **amazed / amazing** by all the shops and restaurants.

Hong: That sounds good. Are your neighbors friendly?

Karine: Well, I'm not sure. I am a little **frustrated / frustrating** because no one says hello.

But there is a block party next week, so that will be **interested / interesting**.

Hong: A block party? That sounds fun.

Karine: Yeah. My son is very **excited / exciting**. He really wants to meet some other kids.

Hong: Are there any other children in your building?

Karine: No. My son was very **disappointed / disappointing** about that.

C **Complete the sentences. Use the *-ed* or *-ing* form of the verbs in the box.**

> confuse   disappoint   embarrass
> ~~excite~~   frighten   interest

1. Moving to a new neighborhood is hard, but it's ___exciting___ to meet new people.

2. I had met the woman many times, but I forgot her name! I was so _____!

3. Amy was looking forward to the festival. She was _____ when it was cancelled.

4. Our neighborhood isn't safe. People are _____ to go out at night.

5. Could you please explain how to fill out this form? I'm a little _____.

6. Are you _____ in going to the community center tonight to see a movie?

D **Read the paragraph. Correct four more mistakes with participial adjectives and prepositions.**

   When my grandparents moved into a new apartment building, they were a little worried ~~for~~ _about_ the neighbors. There were a lot of teenagers who were loud and a little frightened. One night, my grandparents got back home and realized they didn't have their apartment keys. They were too embarrassing to knock on a neighbor's door and ask for help. Suddenly, a teenage boy came into the building. He was big and scary-looking. My grandmother was terrified. Then, the boy smiled and offered to help them. He called the building manager on his cell phone and waited until they got into their apartment. My grandparents were surprised for his kindness, and very relieved! Since then, the boy stops over regularly to see if he can help my grandparents. He isn't so terrified after all.

LIFE SKILLS

A Look at the map. Read the directions. Where is the party being held? Write the name of the location on the invitation.

NEIGHBORHOOD PARTY!

Saturday, September 23rd   **3 PM – 6 PM** _____ Park

Coming from the east:

1. Take Route 120 west to South Union Road.

2. Take the exit for South Union Road.

3. Drive north on South Union Road to Wawona Street.

4. Turn right on Wawona Street.

5. Drive east 2 blocks until you see the park on your right.

B Rewrite the directions to the party for someone coming from the west on Route 120.

Coming from the west:

1. _Take Route 120 east to Locust Avenue._ _____

2. _____

3. _____

4. _____

5. _____

C On notepaper, write driving directions from your home to your English class.

DICTIONARY SKILL: Understand words with more than one meaning

A Read the dictionary entry for the word *service*. Write one example phrase or sentence from the dictionary for each meaning.

---

ser•vice¹ /'sɚvɪs/ *n.*

1 IN A STORE ETC. [U] the help that people who work in a restaurant, hotel, store etc. give you: *The food is terrific but the service is lousy.* | the **customer service** department

2 WORK DONE [C,U] the work that you do for someone or an organization: *He retired after 20 years of service.* | *You may need the services of a lawyer.* | *She was given an award in honor of her years of service to the Democratic Party.*

3 BUSINESS [C] a business that provides help or does jobs for people rather than producing things: *a cleaning service*

4 public services things such hospitals, schools, etc. that are provided by the government for the public to use: *The new budget will cut city services such as trash collection and library hours.*

Source: *Longman Dictionary of American English*

1 IN A STORE ETC: _____

2 WORK DONE: _____

3 BUSINESS: _____

4 public services: _____

B Which meaning of *service* is being used in each sentence? Write the number.

1. Today we honor Judy Lee for her many years of service to our club. _____

2. My husband works for an Internet service provider. _____

3. We need better community services in my neighborhood. _____

4. Veronica started her own housecleaning service. _____

5. If we want to give our customers faster service, we'll have to hire more cashiers. _____

6. Because of the hurricane, many towns near the coast do not have mail service. _____

7. That store needs to improve its customer service—the sales clerks are not very helpful. _____

Ⓐ **Complete the conversation. Use the conditional. More than one answer is possible.**

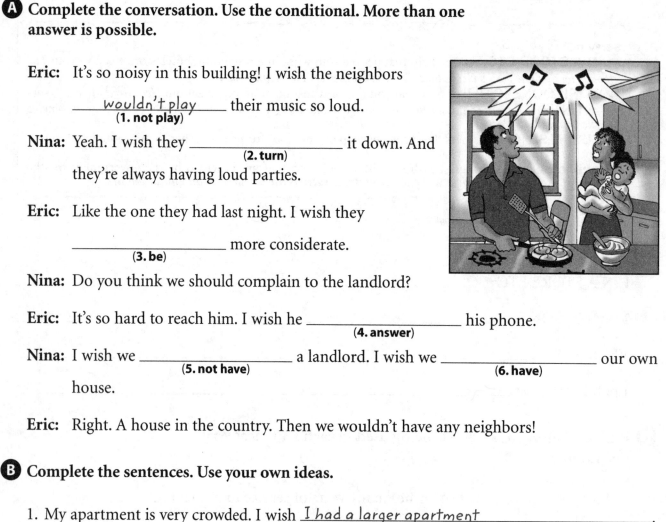

Eric: It's so noisy in this building! I wish the neighbors

_____wouldn't play_____ their music so loud.
(**1. not play**)

Nina: Yeah. I wish they _____ it down. And
(**2. turn**)

they're always having loud parties.

Eric: Like the one they had last night. I wish they

_____ more considerate.
(**3. be**)

Nina: Do you think we should complain to the landlord?

Eric: It's so hard to reach him. I wish he _____ his phone.
(**4. answer**)

Nina: I wish we _____ a landlord. I wish we _____ our own
(**5. not have**)   (**6. have**)

house.

Eric: Right. A house in the country. Then we wouldn't have any neighbors!

Ⓑ **Complete the sentences. Use your own ideas.**

1. My apartment is very crowded. I wish _I had a larger apartment_____.

2. There isn't a place for Eva's children to play. She wishes _____.

3. Adam doesn't know any of his neighbors. He wishes _____.

4. Hong has to drive a long way to work. He wishes _____.

5. My daughter's friends live a long way away. She wishes _____.

6. Phuong doesn't have anything to do during the day. She wishes _____.

7. Mei-Yu is afraid to go out of her house after dark. She wishes _____.

8. Dmitry can never find a place to park. He wishes _____.

C Look at the picture. What does each person wish? Write a sentence for each person.

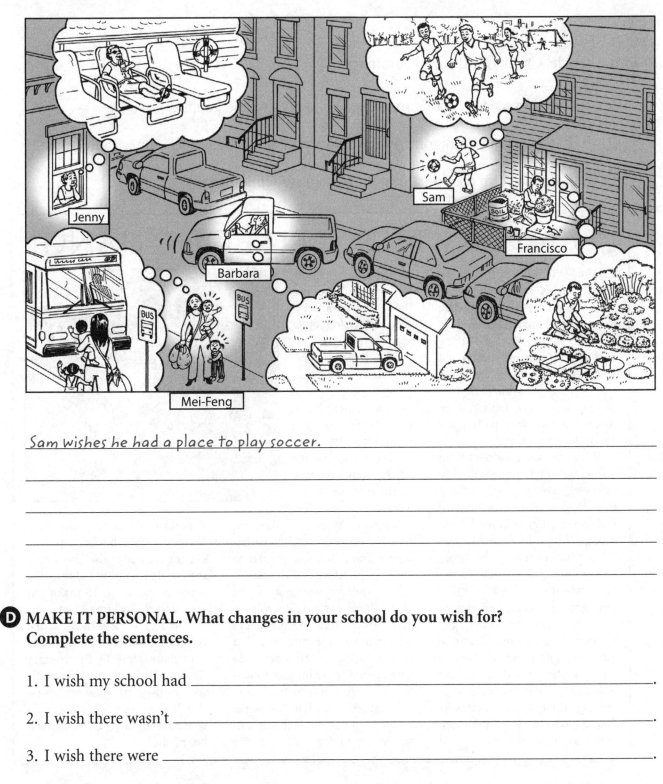

Sam wishes he had a place to play soccer.

_____

_____

_____

_____

D MAKE IT PERSONAL. What changes in your school do you wish for? Complete the sentences.

1. I wish my school had _____.

2. I wish there wasn't _____.

3. I wish there were _____.

4. I wish my teacher would _____.

READ

Read the article. Check (✓) the best summary.

_____ a. Catalino started a gardening business to help young people.

_____ b. Catalino is an immigrant who worked hard and achieved the American dream.

_____ c. Catalino started an organization to help students succeed.

PLANTING THE SEEDS OF CHANGE

Catalino Tapia came to the United States as a young man with six dollars in his pocket. He worked hard and eventually started his own gardening business. He married and bought a comfortable home in Redwood City, California, with a view of San Francisco Bay. Tapia and his wife raised two sons, putting the eldest through college.

When his son graduated from law school, Tapia was inspired to help other young people make it to college, although he himself had never studied beyond sixth grade. With help from his son, Tapia **established** a nonprofit corporation—the Gardeners **Foundation**—and asked other immigrant gardeners to help him.

Tapia began by asking the wealthy clients of his gardening business for **donations**. In just two weeks, he had raised $10,000 for scholarships, and the money kept coming. The Bay Area Gardeners Foundation now gives a minimum of ten scholarships each year and provides information to students about how they can continue their education after high school.

"I believe the education of our young people isn't just the responsibility of their parents, especially in the Latino community where some parents work two or three jobs," says Tapia.

Gloria Escobar, nineteen, received one of the scholarships. Gloria knew that she wanted to study architecture, but the classes that she needed were not offered at her local community college. The money from the gardener's fund allowed her to travel to a college farther away where she could earn the credits she needed to transfer to a university.

Another **recipient**, Alberto Urieta, hopes to major in molecular biology. "To receive a scholarship is so much help because the books are so expensive, but it also gives us a feeling that we're not alone, that someone wants us to make our dreams a reality," says Urieta.

Tapia understands that children who are educated can contribute more to the country than those who are not. "It's a little seed we're planting," he said. "And it will eventually grow a garden of students, and it will flower and **bear** fruit."

Source: www.bagf.org

CHECK YOUR UNDERSTANDING

A **Read the article again. Answer the questions.**

1. What did Catalino Tapia do for a living? _____

2. Why did he establish the Gardeners Foundation? _____

3. Where did the money for the foundation originally come from? _____

4. What does the foundation do? _____

5. How did the foundation help Gloria Escobar? _____

B **Make inferences. Read the statements. Circle _True_ or _False_.**

> **Reading Skill:**
> Making Inferences
>
> If an author doesn't give information directly, use what you read to make a logical guess about what is probably true.

1. Catalino Tapia was poor when he arrived in the U.S.   **True**   **False**

2. Tapia's gardening business did not succeed.   **True**   **False**

3. Tapia is proud of his son.   **True**   **False**

4. Tapia's clients did not want to help.   **True**   **False**

5. The students who receive scholarships are mainly Latino.   **True**   **False**

6. The students' parents are wealthy.   **True**   **False**

C **WORD WORK. Find the boldface words in the article. Then match the words with the definitions. Write the letter on the line.**

1. ____ **establish**

2. ____ **foundation**

3. ____ **donation**

4. ____ **recipient**

5. ____ **bear (fruit)**

a. a person who receives something

b. to produce

c. to start or set up something

d. an organization that collects money for charity

e. money that is given to a person or organization

A Read the pamphlet. Underline the examples of verb + object + infinitive.

VOTE
TOM HALL
FOR GREENVILLE CITY COUNCIL

Dear friend,
I <u>am asking you to vote</u> for me. Why? You expect your politicians to know your neighborhood. I have lived and worked in this city for twenty years. You want the city to improve services. As your representative, I will urge the city to expand after-school programs for our children. I will ask the city council to increase funding for street cleaning and recycling programs. Remind your neighbors to vote on November 4. Tell them to vote for me!

B Rewrite the sentences. Change the underlined words to pronouns.

1. The politician asked <u>my husband and me</u> to vote for him.

   The politician asked us to vote for him.

2. The instructor taught <u>Robert</u> to resist an attack.

   _____

3. We didn't expect <u>Mrs. Santiago</u> to call a meeting.

   _____

4. How would you like <u>your neighbors</u> to help you?

   _____

5. The police officers encouraged <u>my neighbors and me</u> to start a community group.

   _____

6. We're advising <u>you and your family</u> to lock your doors.

   _____

C Read Officer Saland's safety tips. Restate her advice using the verb in parentheses + object + infinitive. Make any other necessary changes.

1. "Keep your eyes open."

   (**urge**) _Officer Saland urged us to keep our eyes open._

2. "Call the police if you see anything suspicious."

   (**would like**) _____

3. "Don't carry a lot of cash."

   (**advise**) _____

Officer Saland

4. "If possible, walk home with a friend."

   (**encourage**) _____

5. "Walk in well-lit areas."

   (**tell**) _____

6. "Stay aware of your surroundings, especially at night."

   (**remind**) _____

D Read the community problems. Suggest a way to solve each problem. Complete the sentence with your own idea. Use an object + infinitive.

1. **Problem:** Teens in our neighborhood can't find jobs, so they get in trouble.

   Solution: Job-skills training classes will help _teens to find jobs_____.

2. **Problem:** Seniors are often easy targets for crime.

   Solution: Organize self-defense classes that will teach _____.

3. **Problem:** The residents in our apartment building don't know each other.

   Solution: Hold a potluck party that will encourage _____.

4. **Problem:** Children run into the street without looking.

   Solution: Parents should warn _____.

A Complete the paragraph. Use the sentences in the box.

> My bank is around the corner, and there is even a
>   post office just a few blocks away.
> My neighbors always say hello and ask me how
>   I'm doing when I walk by.
> People walk to and from the subway, even quite
>   late at night.

Writing Tip

Details are important in your writing. Examples are an excellent way to give details.

I live near Twelfth Avenue. It's a very busy area, but that's why I like it! It's always full of

people. (1.) _____

_____ Also, there are always a lot of people going to the restaurants and bars.

Another reason I like my neighborhood is because I don't need a car—I can walk everywhere!

There is an excellent market that has most of the food that I need, and a hardware store.

(2.) _____

_____ Finally, it's easy to meet people in my neighborhood. Neighbors are

often sitting in front of their houses watching their children or just relaxing outside.

(3.) _____

B Read the student paragraph. Correct five more mistakes.

When my wife and I first came to this neighborhood, we were ~~disappointing~~ *disappointed*. There was
a lot garbage on the street and graffiti. We wished that the street looks nicer. But then we
formed a neighborhood group and we asked people joining us. At first people weren't
interesting, but little by little they volunteered to help. We cleaned up the graffiti and planted
trees on the sidewalk. Now the streets look much better, and we are very exciting about what
we have achieved. I would encourage everybody doing what we did. It really works!

A How many more words can you think of? Add to each list.

Neighborhood problems	Things at a street fair
graffiti	music
potholes	crafts
trash	entertainment

Learning Strategy:
List Connected Words

Help yourself remember vocabulary by listing all the words you know connected with a topic.

B Make compound nouns. Use the words in the box.

center   citizens   collection   ~~council~~   field   programs

1. city ___council___

2. baseball _____

3. senior _____

4. after-school _____

5. community _____

6. trash _____

C Complete the paragraph. Use the compound nouns from Exercise B.

The (1.) ___city council___ is improving the park in our neighborhood. It is

making a new playground and (2.) _____. It is also building a new

(3.) _____ that will offer (4.) _____ for children and social

activities for (5.) _____. In addition, it will schedule more frequent

(6.) _____ to keep the park clean.

A **Complete the conversations. Use the words in the box.**

> count on   ~~figure out~~   get over   hand out
> help out   point out   put together   show up

1. **A:** Can you show me how to set up the fax machine?

   B: I'll try, but I don't know if I can _____figure_____ it _____out_____.

2. **A:** I think Samuel is upset that he didn't get the job.

   B: I'm sure he is, but he'll _____ it. In a few days he'll feel better.

3. **A:** Can you _____ the new supervisor?

   B: That's her, over in the corner. She has blond hair and wears glasses.

4. **A:** We've got a lot to do to finish this project.

   B: You can _____ me to help as much as possible.

5. **A:** What do we need to do to finish?

   B: We need to _____ a final report and then we're done.

6. **A:** Do you like working with Marta?

   B: Yes, she's always willing to _____ when you need it.

7. **A:** Kevin didn't _____ for his shift last night.

   B: I'll call him. It isn't like him to miss work and not notify someone.

8. **A:** Can I help with anything at the orientation meeting?

   B: Yes, thanks. Take these W-2 forms and employee handbooks and _____

   them _____ to each new employee.

B Complete the phrasal verbs. Use the particles in the box. Some particles may be used more than once.

> off   on   out   over   together   up

1. Who helped you put _____together_____ this report? It's very well done.

2. Mike is upset that his coworker got a promotion and he didn't, but he'll get _____ it.

3. I couldn't figure _____ what to do next, but Min-Ji helped me.

4. Don't forget to turn _____ the computer and printer when you're finished.

5. Bruno didn't show _____ for his shift last night. Is something wrong?

6. Could you please look at this and point _____ any mistakes?

7. We need to have a meeting to talk _____ these new company policies.

8. Elsa wants to take a vacation next month. She is counting _____ us to manage the store while she is gone.

C Rewrite the sentences. Replace the underlined words with the pronouns *her*, *him*, *it*, or *them*.

1. Javier and I talked over <u>the office procedures</u>. _____*Javier and I talked them over.*_____

2. We figured out <u>the accounting problem</u>. _____

3. Could you please help <u>Beatriz</u> out? She's new. _____

4. I put together <u>the documents</u> for the new project. _____

5. Let's bring up <u>that issue</u> at the staff meeting. _____

6. I signed <u>Jim</u> up for extra shifts. He wants more hours. _____

7. We looked up <u>that procedure</u> in the policy manual. _____

LIFE SKILLS

A Look at the company bulletin board. Read the notices about benefits. Check (✓) the topics that are mentioned.

❑ working overtime   ❑ dates for being paid

❑ changing your dental plan   ❑ paid time off

❑ holiday time off   ❑ vacation request forms

Notice:

- All overtime **must** be approved by your supervisor.
- Talk to your supervisor as soon as you know you might be working overtime.
- You are allowed to work a maximum of seven hours of overtime per week.
- Remember, if overtime hours are not approved, you will **not** be paid!

Deadline for changes to health benefits

You must make changes to your medical and dental benefits plan before April 30. During this open enrollment period you may:

• Choose a different medical or dental plan
• Remove a family member from your plan
• Add a family member to your plan

CHANGE IN PAID TIME OFF

After ninety days of employment, all full-time employees are now eligible for the following paid time off (PTO):

Sick days:
5 sick days per year

Vacation days
The number of vacation days is now based on length of service:

90 days–2 years:	5 days
3–4 years:	8 days
5–9 years:	10 days
10 years or more:	12 days

You must request vacation days at least two weeks in advance. Please submit a *Vacation Request Form* to your supervisor for approval.

Read the notices again. Read the statements. Circle *True* or *False*.

1. Employees must ask their supervisor for permission to work overtime. **True** **False**

2. Employees can work eight overtime hours in a week. **True** **False**

3. Employees cannot change health benefits after April 30. **True** **False**

4. After ten years, employees get twelve vacation days. **True** **False**

5. Employees must submit a form to take a sick day. **True** **False**

STUDY SKILL: Use a bar graph

Look at the bar graph. Answer the questions.

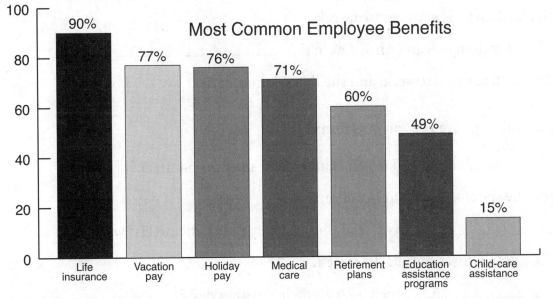

Most Common Employee Benefits

Source: *U.S. Bureau of Labor Statistics*

1. Which type of benefit is offered by the most employers? _____

2. Which is offered by the fewest employers? _____

3. What percentage of employers offer retirement plans? _____

4. What percentage of employers help employees pay for school? _____

5. Which benefit is offered by 71 percent of employers? _____

6. Which benefit is offered by 77 percent of employers? _____

A Unscramble the sentences. Write negative *yes* / *no* questions.

1. **A:** (you / didn't / work / on Monday) <u>Didn't you work on Monday?</u>

   B: No, I didn't. I worked on Tuesday.

2. **A:** (have / a uniform / wear / you / don't / to) _____

   B: No, I don't. There's no company dress code.

3. **A:** (they / yet / opened / haven't / the store) _____

   B: No, they don't open until nine o'clock.

4. **A:** (start / new job / he / his / last week / didn't) _____

   B: No, he didn't. He starts in two weeks.

5. **A:** (she / a training session / had / hasn't) _____

   B: Yes, she had one last week, and she'll have another next week.

B Complete the negative *yes* / *no* questions.

1. **A:** _____<u>Shouldn't</u>_____ Tina clock out when she goes on break?

   B: Yes, she should. I'll talk to her about that.

2. **A:** _____ you read the company policy memo last week?

   B: No, I didn't. I was out sick last week.

3. **A:** _____ they used all their vacation days?

   B: No, they haven't. I think they have a few days left.

4. **A:** _____ you finish that paperwork tomorrow?

   B: No, I can't. It has to be finished by the end of the day.

5. **A:** _____ he already learned that procedure?

   B: He has, but he wants to review it.

6. **A:** _____ the new employees attending this meeting?

   B: No, they aren't. They have a different meeting tomorrow.

C Complete the conversations. Write negative questions.

1. **A:** My new job isn't going very well.

   B: Why not? _Didn't you get the position you wanted?_
   (**you / did get the position you wanted**)

   A: Not exactly. I wanted to be a server, but I'm washing dishes instead.

   B: That's too bad. _____
   (**you / did tell them you wanted to be a server**)

   A: Well, yes, but they need dishwashers right now.

2. **A:** I want to go to the party on Saturday, but I have to work.

   B: Oh no! _____
   (**you / did tell your boss you needed that night off**)

   A: Yes, but I'm on the schedule.

   B: _____
   (**someone else / can work**)

   A: I don't know. I'm going to find out.

D Read the statements. Write negative *yes / no* questions to ask about things you think might be true. More than one answer is possible.

1. **A:** I don't know how to complete this paperwork.

   B: (supervisor tell you) _Didn't your supervisor tell you how to do it?_

2. **A:** Pavel had work until 11 P.M. last night.

   B: (usually finish by 7 P.M.) _____

3. **A:** I forgot to clock out when I finished work yesterday.

   B: (tell your supervisor) _____

4. **A:** They cleaned the kitchen when they got into work this morning.

   B: (usually clean at night) _____

5. **A:** We all have to work extra shifts next month.

   B: (hire more workers) _____

6. **A:** I'm so tired. I haven't stopped working since seven o'clock.

   B: (take a break) _____

READ

Read the article. Check (✓) the workplace injuries discussed.

❑ strains   ❑ sprains   ❑ burns   ❑ repetitive motion injuries   ❑ falls

How to Avoid Workplace Injuries

About 6 million workers suffer **non-fatal** workplace injuries and illnesses each year, which can cost businesses billions of dollars. Workplace injuries and illnesses are often caused by unsafe work practices, hazardous conditions, or exposures to harmful chemicals. Here we take a look at some of the causes of injury and how to prevent them.

More than 40 percent of workplace injuries are strains and sprains caused by **excessive** lifting, pushing, or pulling; or by carrying heavy objects. According to the National Safety Council, **improper** lifting and carrying heavy objects can cause serious injuries. When you use safe lifting techniques, you are less likely to suffer from back strain, pulled muscles, and other complaints.

It's not just heavy lifting that causes injury. Repeated motions associated with certain workplace tasks, such as typing on a computer keyboard or working on an assembly line, can result in medical conditions, too. To avoid repetitive motion injuries, make sure you take breaks throughout the day. If you sit in a chair for long periods of time, make sure you stand up and **stretch** regularly. Also, maintain correct **posture** by having materials, tools and equipment a comfortable distance from your body.

Injuries in the workplace can also result from workers falling on slippery surfaces. To avoid falls, clean any wet areas immediately and be sure that workers wear proper footwear.

Finally, studies show that 18 percent of all injuries in the workplace are the result of fatigue. Being overtired creates a risk to employees who do work that requires concentration and quick response. Getting enough sleep can help prevent injuries because of fatigue. Remember, it's important to get seven to eight hours of sleep a night.

Source: U.S. Bureau of Labor Statistics

CHECK YOUR UNDERSTANDING

A Read the article again. Answer the questions.

1. What are three causes of workplace injuries? _____

2. What types of injuries are caused by heavy lifting? _____

3. What are two ways to prevent falls? _____

4. How much sleep does the article recommend to avoid fatigue? _____

B Find the following sentences in the article. Then find another sentence in the article that has a similar meaning. Write the sentence on the line.

> **Reading Skill:**
> Recognizing Restatements
>
> When you read, look for information that the author repeats or explains again with different words.

1. More than 40 percent of workplace injuries are

   strains and sprains caused by excessive lifting,

   pushing, or pulling; or by carrying heavy objects.

   _____

2. To avoid repetitive motion injuries, make sure you take breaks throughout the day.

   _____

C WORD WORK. Find the boldface words in the article. Complete the sentences. Circle the letters.

1. When something is **non-fatal**, it means _____.
   a. it results in death
   b. it doesn't result in death

2. If something is **excessive**, it _____.
   a. is more than is needed
   b. is painful

3. Something that is **improper** is _____.
   a. correct or acceptable
   b. not correct or acceptable

4. When you **stretch**, you _____.
   a. sprain your muscles
   b. make your muscles looser

5. Your **posture** is the way you _____.
   a. hold your body when you sit or stand
   b. repeat the same motions

A Complete the paragraph. Circle the correct words.

Our manager asked the team **work** / (**to work**) faster. She **said** / **advised** us, "We aren't meeting our quotas. We all need to speed up." We asked her **suggest** / **to suggest** ways to work faster. We **said** / **told**, "We don't know how to work faster." She told us **help** / **to help** each other more. She **said** / **told** us, "If you help each other out, you'll work faster and meet your quotas." But, she also reminded us **not forget** / **not to forget** about safety. She **said** / **warned** us, "It's easy to forget about safety when you work quickly."

B Complete Yolanda's e-mail to summarize a training session.

Hi Brian,

Here's what we did in our training today: First, the instructor _____asked us to summarize_____
(1. ask / us / summarize)
yesterday's training session. That was hard because I couldn't remember everything!

Then, he _____ in groups and review the employee handbook. He
(2. tell / us / work)

_____ our group, so I'm glad I read the handbook last night! He
(3. ask / me / lead)

_____ any questions we had about the handbook. Our group had
(4. say / write down)

a lot of questions. After that, he _____ everyone's questions. That
(5. ask / the group / discuss)

was really useful. I took notes for you on that. He _____ our notes
(6. advise / everyone / review)

before our first shift. Let me know if you have questions!

Yolanda

C Read a supervisor's instructions to a group of new employees. Rewrite her direct commands. Use indirect speech.

1. Please arrive on time. (**tell**) _She told us to arrive on time._

2. Wear comfortable clothes. (**tell**) _____

3. Don't wear jeans. (**ask**) _____

4. Check the information sheet every day. (**say**) _____

5. Wash your hands before starting a shift. (**instruct**) _____

6. Take a twenty-minute break every shift. (**say**) _____

7. Please don't take a longer break. (**ask**) _____

8. Sign your time card at the end of a shift. (**remind**) _____

D Read a student's journal entry about her first day on the job. Correct five more mistakes.

I was really nervous when I first started working as a server at Kip's Restaurant. My boss,
Terry, told me not ^to worry, but it was hard. Terry ask me to start by watching him take an order.
He said me to pay attention to how he wrote everything down. It seemed really easy when I
watched him do it! Then, he asked to take the next order. He advised me repeat the order
back to the customer to make sure it was correct. And, he reminded me not be nervous. Of
course I was, but the customer was very nice, and I didn't forget anything!

A Read the office memo. Write a subject line.

Writing Tip

Memos should always include a subject line.

Memo **HIGH TECH SALES**

To: Siliva Gao, Department Supervisor
From: Leon Portero, Sales Associate
Date: 10/24/10
Re: _____

Recently we had a meeting to talk about ways that we can make our office more environmentally friendly. One area I think we can improve on is our use of paper. I am writing this memo to suggest two ideas.

- **Set the copiers to print on both sides of the paper.** Most employees only print on one side. Printing on both sides would cut our paper usage by 50 percent.

- **Put a paper recycling bin next to every copier.** Most of the paper we use is thrown away in the regular wastebaskets. We only have one recycling bin for paper and it is near the mailroom. If we place one paper recycling bin near each copy machine, more paper will be recycled.

Thank you for considering these suggestions. I hope that we can discuss them at our next meeting.

B Read the office memo. Correct four more mistakes.

In our last meeting, we discuss~~ed~~ the problem of keeping the restaurant kitchen clean. Here is some suggestions to solve this problem:

- Cooks shouldn't wait until the end of a shift to cleaning. We should to train new cooks to clean as they cook.

- We should schedule one cook to stay longer to clean at the end of each shift.

- We should assign one person to supervise and approve all cleaning.

Thank you for consider my suggestions. I hope we can discuss them next week.

A Match the nouns that commonly go together.

1. __f__ warehouse   a. problem

2. ____ performance   b. construction

3. ____ road   c. injury

4. ____ employee   d. benefits

5. ____ delivery   e. review

6. ____ workplace   f. manager

> **Learning Strategy:**
> Use Collocation
>
> A *collocation* is an arrangement of words that usually go together. Practice learning words that are often used together to increase your vocabulary.

B Choose the noun that goes with each verb.

1. ask for   (a.) clarification   b. issues

2. meet   a. quotas   b. delays

3. follow   a. time   b. instructions

4. solve   a. problems   b. clarification

5. spend   a. time   b. instructions

6. avoid   a. time   b. delays

C Complete the sentences. Use expressions from Exercise B.

1. It's important to _ask for clarification_ if you don't understand something.

2. Salespeople who _____ their _____ usually get a bonus.

3. I told Mike how to prepare the report, but he didn't _____

   my _____.

4. We all go to Yolanda for help when we need to _____. She can fix anything.

5. I sent the important package by overnight mail to _____.

6. I need to _____ cleaning my files this morning. They're a mess!

A Complete the sentences. Match the beginnings with the endings.

1. If you live in an apartment building, __g__

2. Call 911 and leave the building ____

3. Turn off the stove ____

4. If you have children, ____

5. If a pan catches fire, ____

6. If someone in your household is a smoker, ____

7. A fire can get out of control ____

a. teach them about the dangers of fire.

b. if you don't act quickly.

c. if you have to leave the kitchen.

d. ask them to smoke outside.

e. cover it and turn off the stove.

f. if you have a fire in your home.

g. you should know where the exits are.

B Combine the two clauses to make a conditional sentence about fire safety. Keep the same order and decide which clause begins with *if*. Include a comma if necessary.

1. (you should know what to do / there is an emergency)

   You should know what to do if there is an emergency.

2. (you smell smoke / call the fire department)

   _____

3. (you hear the fire alarm / you need to evacuate the building)

   _____

4. (don't panic / you have to evacuate)

   _____

5. (you might be in danger / you don't act quickly)

   _____

C Look at the pictures. On notepaper, write advice about what to do in each situation. Use the conditional with an *if* clause and a result clause.

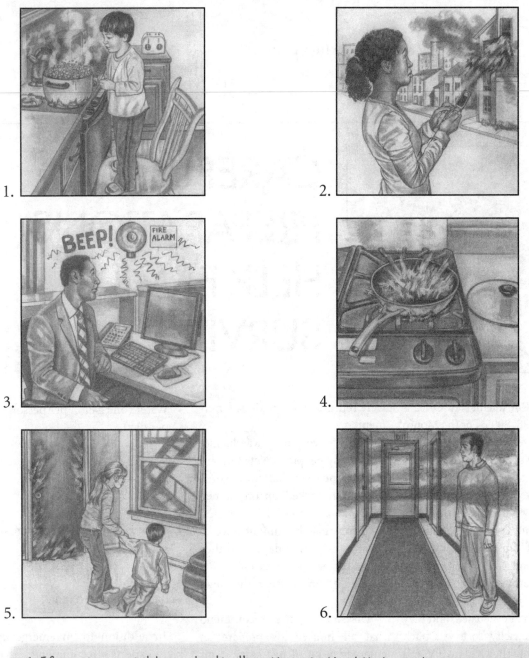

1.

2.

3.

4.

5.

6.

1. If you have children, don't allow them in the kitchen when you are cooking.

D MAKE IT PERSONAL. Write two things that you have learned about fire safety from this unit.

_____

_____

READ

Read the article. Why was the Monro family lucky?

CAREFUL PREPARATIONS HELP FAMILY SURVIVE

Hurricane Katrina hit New Orleans on August 28, 2005. For the Monro family, who stayed behind, it was a frightening experience.

As the rain kept coming, the water started seeping into their home. The Monros moved their TVs and the family computer to a higher floor and sat upstairs, watching the neighborhood slowly flood.

As the family waited for rescue, they felt utterly alone. Their neighbors had evacuated, and they had no electricity, so it was pitch dark at night. They had no TV, and their cell phones stopped working. They realized that the best thing to do would be to wait until help came.

Finally, after five long days, the Monros were rescued. They were flown to Houston, where they were reunited with anxious family members.

The Monro family was luckier than many people in New Orleans because they were better prepared. They had stocked up on canned food and water in advance, knowing that they might have to survive for several days. And they had a battery-powered radio that enabled them to hear the news bulletins.

Disaster experts recommend that all households prepare an emergency kit of necessary items to help them survive during an emergency such as a flood, a tornado, or an earthquake. Remember that you may have to survive for several days without outside help. Your emergency kit might include the following items:

- Water (one gallon per person per day)
- Three-day supply of nonperishable food
- Medications and first aid supplies
- Money, checks, or credit cards
- Bedding or sleeping bags
- Flashlights and batteries
- Battery-operated radio

In addition to an emergency kit, experts recommend that families prepare a disaster plan in advance. Agree on where you are going to go and who you are going to contact if disaster strikes. Being prepared in this way can mean the difference between life and death.

CHECK YOUR UNDERSTANDING

A What is the purpose of the article?

    a. to entertain by telling a story

    b. to help readers prepare for emergencies

    c. to give information about emergency kits

B Read the article again. Answer the questions.

1. Where was the Monro family on August 28, 2005?

    _____

2. What happened to the Monro's home? _____

3. What did the family do while they were waiting? _____

4. How long did the family wait to be rescued? _____

5. Where did the family go after they were rescued? _____

6. What are four things you can do to prepare for a disaster? _____

    _____

> **Reading Skill:**
> Identifying an Author's Purpose
>
> Think about an author's goal or purpose. Is it to entertain you by telling you a story? Is it to inform you by giving facts? Is it to persuade you to agree with a specific opinion?

C MAKE IT PERSONAL. Does your household have an emergency kit? What would you do in an emergency?

_____

_____

D WORD WORK. Read each description. Find the word in the article. Write it.

1. a word in paragraph 2 that means "flowing slowly through small holes": _____

2. a word in paragraph 3 that means "completely": _____

3. a word in paragraph 4 that means "brought together again": _____

4. a word in paragraph 5 that means "bought in advance": _____

5. a word in paragraph 5 that means "short news reports": _____

A **Read the weather report. Underline five more time clauses.**

Good evening, folks. Well, it looks like this wet weather will continue <u>until we get to the weekend</u>. But things will get better after this front has passed. It will be drier next week, but it'll be cooler, too, so you may want to take a warm jacket when you go to work on Monday.

We're also getting reports of some flooding in the northern parts of the state, so if you're heading up that way, check the forecast before you head out. We will let you know what's happening up there as soon as we have more information.

I'll be back with more weather after we've had the sports news, so stay tuned!

B **Complete the paragraph. Circle the correct time words and phrases.**

I didn't know there was a tornado coming. I watched the news (before)/ until I went to work, but I didn't hear anything about a tornado watch. But **before / when** I was at work, someone turned on the TV. I didn't pay a lot of attention **as soon as / until** I heard someone say, "There's a tornado in Somerville!" That's where I live. So **as soon as / before** I heard that, I stopped working and watched the news report. It said that parts of the town had been damaged. I waited **until / when** the danger was over, and then I drove home. **Until / When** I got to my house, my wife was waiting for me. She was fine, and so was the house. So we went out to check on our neighbors. **Before / When** we saw what had happened to some people, we realized how lucky we were.

C Complete the paragraph. Use the words in the box.

> after   as soon as   before   until   ~~when~~

(1.) _____ When _____ Rita Montero and her
husband Alvaro heard the hurricane warning, they
quickly boarded up all the windows and doors.

(2.) _____ they left home, they packed two
suitcases. The couple left the area (3.) _____
they were ready. They stayed in a motel
(4.) _____ it was safe to return home.
(5.) _____ the hurricane was over, Alvaro and Rita decided to move to a
different area.

D Complete the sentences. Use your own ideas.

1. If there is a tornado watch, check the weather forecast before ___ *you leave your home* ___.

2. Discuss an emergency plan with your family before _____.

3. As soon as you hear a tornado warning, _____.

4. When a hurricane is predicted, _____.

5. In an earthquake, stay under cover until _____.

6. After a weather emergency is over, _____.

E MAKE IT PERSONAL. Describe an experience you have had with bad
weather or a weather emergency. What happened? What did you do?

_____

_____

_____

LIFE SKILLS

A Look at the national weather map and the five-day forecast. Answer the questions.

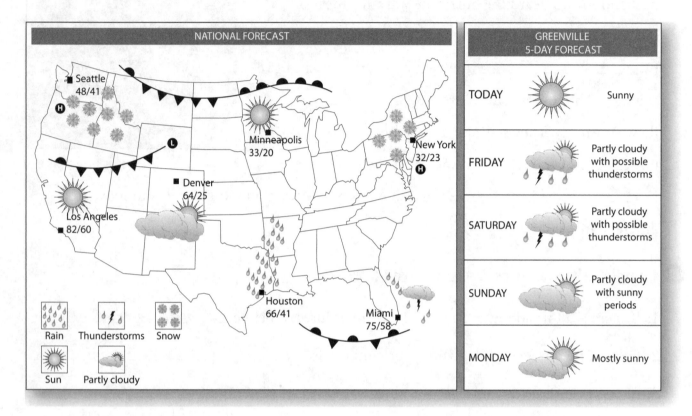

1. Which cities are going to have snow? _____

2. How will the weather be in Denver? _____

3. Which cities are expecting clear, sunny weather? _____

4. Which city might have thunderstorms? _____

5. Which city is likely to have the highest temperature? _____

6. Which city is expecting the lowest temperature? _____

7. What is the weather like in Greenville today? _____

8. Which day is likely to be sunnier in Greenville, Sunday or Monday? _____

B MAKE IT PERSONAL. What is the weather like in your area today?

_____

_____

STUDY SKILL: Use a table

Look at the table. Answer the questions.

CITY	YESTERDAY HI/LO	PCP	TODAY HI/LO	COND	CITY	YESTERDAY HI/LO	PCP	TODAY HI/LO	COND
Atlanta	55/39		56/40	PC	Honolulu	82/72	1.5	79/74	RN
Boston	35/32		48/39	PC	Houston	72/58	.9	74/53	TS
Cincinnati	48/34		43/29	RN	Las Vegas	71/45		71/48	PC
Chicago	45/29	1.7	37/27	SN	Miami	75/64		77/65	S
Dallas	63/49	.2	66/41	PC	Minneapolis	33/20		35/19	SN

PCP: precipitation (rain) **COND**: conditions **PC**: partly cloudy **RN**: rain **S**: sun **SN**: snow **TS**: thunderstorms

1. Which city had the highest temperature yesterday and today? _____

2. Which city had the lowest temperature on both days? _____

3. Which city had the most rain? _____

4. How many cities on the list had no rain at all yesterday? _____

5. What is the most common weather predicted for today? _____

6. Which city on the list might have thunderstorms today? _____

7. How is Cincinnati's weather different today from yesterday? _____

8. Will it be cooler or warmer today than yesterday in Boston? _____

9. Imagine you are going to Miami. Will you need an umbrella? _____

A Match the sentences that go together. Write the letter.

1. Please answer the phone. _c_

2. The traffic is backed up. ____

3. Let's listen to the weather forecast. ____

4. Speak loudly. ____

5. Don't move him. ____

6. Beatriz isn't at work today. ____

7. That guy looks like Ivan. ____

a. Could he be his brother?

b. He might be injured.

c. It might be an important call.

d. It could rain later.

e. She must be sick.

f. There must be an accident up ahead.

g. They might not hear you.

B Read the conversations. Rewrite the underlined sentences. Use the words in parentheses.

1. **A:** What's going on over there?

   B: There's an ambulance. <u>I think someone is hurt.</u> (**must**) ___Someone must be hurt___.

   A: I think that's Mrs. Cruz's house. I hope it's not serious.

   B: <u>I don't think it is serious.</u> (**can't**) _____. Look. The EMTs are

   leaving already.

2. **A:** Look. I fell and hurt my hand. It's really swollen.

   B: Are you OK? <u>It probably hurts.</u> (**must**) _____.

   A: It does! <u>Do you think it is broken?</u> (**could**) _____?

   B: No, I don't think so. <u>Maybe it is sprained.</u> (**might**) _____.

3. **A:** Look! Is that smoke?

   B: <u>Maybe it is.</u> (**might**) _____. It looks like it.

   A: <u>Where is it coming from?</u> (**could**) _____?

   B: <u>It is probably a fire.</u> (**must**) _____. I can smell it now.

C **Look at the picture. Write sentences describing the situation. Use** *could (not)*, *may (not)*, *might (not)*, **or** *must (not)*. **Use the words in parentheses and your own ideas.**

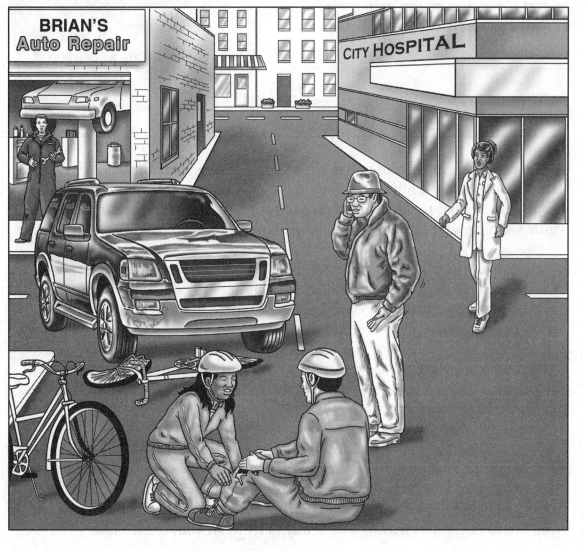

1. (cyclist / hurt) _The cyclist must be hurt._

2. (leg / broken) _____

3. (driver / call) _____

4. (woman / know the cyclist) _____

5. (older woman / a doctor) _____

6. (mechanic / work / auto repair shop) _____

7. (your own idea) _____

8. (your own idea) _____

A Read the text about evacuation preparations.
Number the paragraphs in a logical order.

Writing Tip

When you write about how to do
something, put the steps in the
process in a logical order.

1 | Evacuations happen more often than people realize. Sometimes in a weather emergency, such as a hurricane, you might have a day or two to prepare to leave your home. Other times, in an emergency like a wildfire, you have to leave with little warning, so it is important to be well prepared.

☐ | Next, make sure that you are ready to leave and that your home is secure. Close and lock doors and windows in your home, and unplug most electrical appliances. Keep a battery-powered radio and check it frequently to hear the latest updates and evacuation instructions.

☐ | If you are instructed to leave, gather your family and leave immediately to avoid being trapped by severe weather. Follow recommended evacuation routes. Do not take any shortcuts.

☐ | If you know that an evacuation is likely, here are some things that you can do. First, make sure that you have transportation. If you have a car, fill it up with gas. It is best to take just one car per household. Make sure that you have some emergency supplies with you. Gather emergency food, water, medical supplies, and blankets. Contact friends and family to let them know your plans.

B Read the paragraph. Correct four more mistakes.

It is
~~Is~~ important to agree on a meeting place where everyone in your family can go in
an emergency. That way, everyone knows where go, and family members do not have
to travel around the city to look for each other. It's also a good idea to call out-of-state
friends or family members to let their know you are OK. When is an emergency, the
telephone lines in your local area may not working.

A Match each word or phrase with a word or phrase with the same, but stronger, meaning.

Learning Strategy:
Note Strong Meanings

Some words have strong meanings. Make a note of words that have strong meanings so that you use them appropriately.

1. _h_ bad weather   a. a blizzard

2. ____ cold   b. a downpour

3. ____ hot   c. freezing

4. ____ rain   d. a gale

5. ____ snow   e. a hurricane

6. ____ wind   f. terrifying

7. ____ a storm   g. scorching

8. ____ frightening   h. severe weather

B Complete the sentences. Use the words in the box.

> away from   into   off   out of   ~~over~~
> past   through   toward   under

1. We watched the storm come _____ over _____ the mountains.

2. A tornado passed _____ Oklahoma yesterday, destroying several towns.

3. If there is a tornado warning, get _____ the basement as soon as possible.

4. The firefighters helped the girl get _____ the window.

5. The ambulances often go _____ our house on their way to the hospital.

6. If you feel an earthquake, get _____ a table.

7. Young-Jin fell _____ his bike and hurt his leg.

8. The police officers warned people to move _____ the fire.

9. The tornado was moving _____ them. "Run!" yelled Sam.

A Rewrite the apartment rules. Use (*not*) *required to* or (*not*) *permitted to.*

1. "You pay the electricity bill. You also need to pay a security deposit."

   Tenants are _required to pay the electricity bill_ and to _pay a security deposit_.

2. "You don't have to pay the garbage bill."

   Tenants are _____.

3. "You can have a bird or a fish, but no cats or dogs."

   Tenants are _____, but they are _____.

4. "You need to give one month's notice if you're going to move out."

   Tenants are _____ before moving out.

B Complete the conversation. Use the words in parentheses and *required to*, *allowed to*, or *permitted to.* More than one answer may be possible.

Seung-Ho: I have a few questions about the apartment. I saw that there are storage rooms in

the basement. _____Are we allowed to use_____ them?
                    (1. we / use)

Manager: Yes. _____ one storage room.
                  (2. each tenant / use)

Seung-Ho: OK. And how about parking? We have two cars.

Manager: Well, _____ one parking spot in the lot behind the
                   (3. each tenant / use)
building. So _____ your other car on the street.
              (4. you / park)

Seung-Ho: All right. One last question. My husband is a smoker.

_____ in the building?
(5. he / smoke)

Manager: I'm afraid _____ in the building.
                        (6. tenants / not / smoke)

Seung-Ho: I understand. Actually, that's good. Maybe it'll encourage him to quit smoking!

C Look at the signs showing tenant responsibilities. Write two sentences about each sign. Begin with *You're not allowed to* and *You're supposed to*.

1.

You're not allowed to use this door.

You're supposed to use the other door.

2. _____

_____

3. _____

_____

4. _____

_____

5. _____

_____

6. _____

_____

LIFE SKILLS

A Look at the extract from an apartment lease. Check (✓) the topics that are mentioned.

❏ hanging laundry   ❏ parking rules

❏ the cleaning deposit   ❏ blocked water pipes

❏ changing the door locks   ❏ noise

❏ number of tenants allowed   ❏ lost keys

Rules and Regulations. The tenant will keep the premises in good condition during the term of this agreement. The tenant will

(a) not block the driveways, sidewalks, entryways, stairs and/or halls;

(b) not keep personal belongings such as boxes, furniture, bicycles, and strollers in the common areas of the property, including the basement, hallway, lobby, and stairs;

(c) keep all windows, glass, doors, and locks in good condition;

(d) not hang any laundry, clothing, sheets, etc., from any window, porch or balcony;

(e) not change locks on doors or windows;

(f) keep sinks, toilets, etc., in good working order. The tenant will not put any objects except toilet paper in the toilets. The tenant will pay for any damage to pipes and the cost of clearing pipes that are blocked by misuse;

(g) not make loud noises or otherwise disturb other residents;

(h) deposit all garbage or refuse in the containers provided.

B Look at the lease again. Read the situations. Circle *Yes* or *No*.

1. You have a baby stroller. It is heavy and difficult to carry up the stairs. Can you leave your stroller in the lobby?   **Yes**   **No**

2. You want to buy a stronger lock on your back door. Can you buy and install a new lock?   **Yes**   **No**

3. You'd like to save energy by hanging laundry to dry on the balcony. Are you allowed to do that?   **Yes**   **No**

4. The toilet is blocked. You think your young nephew threw a toy into it. Will you have to pay for a plumber to fix it?   **Yes**   **No**

DICTIONARY SKILL: Identify parts of speech

A Read the dictionary entries for the word *rent*. How is the word used? Circle the correct answer.

a. only as a noun

b. as a noun and a verb

c. as a noun, a verb, and an adjective

> **rent¹** /rɛnt/ *v.* **1** [I,T] to pay money regularly to live in a place that belongs to someone else: *They're renting an apartment near the beach.* | *I rented for years before buying a place.*
> **rent²** *n.* [CU] **1** the amount of money you pay for the use of a house, room, car, etc. that belongs to someone else: *I don't know how we're going to pay the rent next month.*

Source: *Longman Dictionary of American English*

B Read the sentences. Write the correct part of speech (*noun* or *verb*) for each underlined word.

1. How much do you pay in <u>rent</u>?   *noun*

2. Did you pay a security <u>deposit</u> for the apartment?   _____

3. My neighbors are going to <u>move</u> next month.   _____

4. There's a lot of <u>damage</u> in the kitchen.   _____

5. Please <u>deposit</u> the check in the bank.   _____

6. Who's going to <u>rent</u> the apartment now?   _____

7. The <u>move</u> was hard for my grandparents.   _____

8. Please don't <u>damage</u> the new furniture.   _____

A Complete the tag questions. Use the words in the box.

> aren't they   did she   did you   ~~didn't you~~
> doesn't it   is there   isn't he   isn't there

1. You called the plumber, _____didn't you_____?

2. The landlady didn't call, _____?

3. The neighbors are home, _____?

4. There isn't a washing machine in the apartment, _____?

5. The apartment has a dishwasher, _____?

6. The landlord is very helpful, _____?

7. You didn't lose the keys to the apartment, _____?

8. There's a garbage area behind the apartment building, _____?

B Complete the tag questions. Circle the correct words.

1. The people next door are moving out on the fifteenth, **are** / **(aren't)** they?

2. You received my rent check yesterday, **did** / **didn't** you?

3. The building manager is coming to fix the window, **is** / **isn't** he?

4. The washer and dryer work, **do** / **don't** they?

5. The neighbors didn't break the front door lock, **did** / **didn't** they?

6. You complained about the noise last night, **did** / **didn't** you?

7. The landlady wasn't home when you called, **was** / **wasn't** she?

8. We don't have to be home when the plumber comes tomorrow, **do** / **don't** we?

C Complete the conversations. Use tag questions.

1. **A:** It's a nice apartment, _____ isn't it _____?

   B: Yes, it's not bad. You don't think it's too small, _____?

   A: Well, it's a little small, but you don't want to pay more rent, _____?

   B: No, I don't. There's probably enough room.

   A: I think there is.

2. **A:** You don't like the paint in the kitchen, _____?

   B: Not really, but we're allowed to paint, _____?

   A: Yes, I think so. But, it's a lot of work to paint.

   B: Yes, it is, but I don't mind painting on the weekend. You'll help, _____?

   A: Of course.

3. **A:** You like this neighborhood, _____?

   B: Yes, but I'm worried that we can't afford an apartment here. It's an

   expensive area, _____?

   A: Some parts are expensive, but some aren't.

   B: OK, but I'm still worried.

   A: Well, it doesn't hurt to look, _____?

   B: No, you're right. It doesn't.

D Rewrite the sentences. Use question tags.

1. I think we have to fix the window. _We have to fix the window, don't we?_ _____

2. I think James called the landlord. _____

3. This apartment is cold. _____

4. I don't think the neighbors are home. _____

5. The neighborhood is a little noisy. _____

6. I don't think the plumber was here today. _____

7. I think Lola sent in the rent check. _____

READ

Read the article. What made building residents get to know one another?

SUNSET APARTMENTS: NOT JUST A BUILDING

When Elsa and Tim Flores and their daughter moved into their apartment a few years ago, they assumed it was a typical building where neighbors barely knew one another. Instead, over time they realized that they'd found real community at Sunset Apartments.

On the day they moved in, several neighbors came over to introduce themselves. Some brought food for the Flores, and others even offered to help them move boxes and furniture.

The Flores were surprised at how easy it was to meet their neighbors as they **settled into** their new apartment. Tim Flores says, "We've lived in three different buildings and we never got to know any of our neighbors. At Sunset, we met almost everyone within a month."

Elsa was happy to find that several of the mothers had joined together to babysit for one another when they needed it. Soon after they moved in, she had problems with her child care. She was worried she might lose her job because there was no one to care for Marisol, her two-year-old daughter, but some of the other mothers in the building helped her until she found permanent child care. "I really thought I was going to lose my job, but they helped me. Now I help anyone who needs it with their kids," says Elsa.

The apartment building, which houses about fifty families, is located on the edge of North Lambertville. Building manager Vladimir Ivanov says, "People didn't always get along so well in this building. When I first **took over**, no one knew anyone else. We had some terrible crime in the neighborhood, and people were scared. It kind of **forced** them to get to know one another. A few people got together to start a neighborhood watch group and then things changed. Once they knew one another a little, they started **looking out for** one another more. Of course, there are still problems between tenants sometimes, but people try to work them out in a reasonable way.

Tim Flores agrees, "There are always some problems when people live in the same building, but we can usually find a way to **deal with** the problems. It's what makes this place special."

CHECK YOUR UNDERSTANDING

A Read the article again. Check (✓) the main idea of the article.

Reading Skill:
Distinguishing Main Ideas from Details

Use the organization of a text to distinguish an author's main ideas from information that explains or supports those ideas.

❑ At Sunset Apartments, residents introduce themselves and bring food to new residents.

❑ Residents of Sunset Apartments got to know one another after starting a neighborhood watch group.

❑ Sunset Apartments is a special place because residents help one another and work out their problems.

B Read the statements. Circle *True* or *False*.

1. The Flores's earlier building was similar to Sunset Apartments.	True	False
2. The Flores's neighbors offered to help them move in.	True	False
3. The Flores family had trouble getting to know their new neighbors.	True	False
4. Elsa thought she might lose her job because of child care problems.	True	False
5. There are about thirty families in the building.	True	False
6. Vladimir Ivanov is the building manager.	True	False
7. There are never problems between neighbors in the building.	True	False

C WORD WORK. Find the boldface words in the article. Match the words with the definitions.

1. ____ **settle into**   a. to pay attention to and protect someone

2. ____ **take over**   b. to solve a problem

3. ____ **force**   c. to take responsibility for

4. ____ **look out for**   d. to make someone do something

5. ____ **deal with**   e. to begin to feel happy and relaxed in a new situation

A **Complete the story. Use *said* or *told*.**

My friend Sahar called me last week. She was upset because her apartment building used to be quiet, but now it's really noisy. She ___said___ that new neighbors had moved into the
(1.)
apartment below her. The people started having parties late at night. Sahar talked to them and
_____ them that she had to get up really early for work. The new neighbors apologized,
(2.)
and they _____ they would be quiet. But, they started having parties again. Sahar
(3.)
_____ me that she didn't know what to do. I _____ her that she should talk to the
(4.) **(5.)**
landlord, but Sahar _____ she didn't want to cause problems. I _____ her that it
(6.) **(7.)**
would cause even more problems if she lost her job!

B **Arthur complains about his neighbors a lot. Rewrite his complaints. Use *said* and informal English.**

1. "The children are too noisy."

   Arthur said that the children are too noisy.

2. "My rent is too expensive."

   _____

3. "The teenage boy always takes my parking spot."

   _____

4. "My neighbor doesn't take out his trash." _____

5. "I don't like the carpeting in the hallway." _____

6. "My apartment always smells from my neighbors' cooking." _____

7. "The people downstairs always have parties on weekends." _____

8. "The building manager doesn't return my phone calls." _____

C Complete the notes from a residents' meeting.

> ### Riverside Apartments Residents' Meeting   November 24
>
> Mrs. Martinez said that she ___was___ worried about a group of teenagers standing
> (1. be)
>
> outside the front door. Several residents said that they also _____ worried. Mr. Fong
> (2. be)
>
> said that one boy _____ him for money, and he said that he _____ frightened.
> (3. ask)   (4. feel)
>
> Ms. Pari, the building manager, told the residents that she _____ to the police about
> (5. talk)
>
> the situation.
>
> Several residents said that there _____ more noise in the building. Ms. Pari told
> (6. is)
>
> them that she _____ about the problem. She said she _____ to the residents
> (7. know)   (8. talk)
>
> who were making the noise.

D Look at the pictures from a tenants' meeting. Report what each person said.
Complete the sentences.

1. Mrs. Yoon said that ___someone was___

   ___leaving the front door open.___

2. Ms. Price said that _____

   _____.

3. Mr. Kotov said that _____

   _____.

4. The building manager told the residents

   _____.

A Read a tenant's letter of complaint to a landlord (Letter 1). Underline the problem and the solution.

B Read another tenant's letter of complaint (Letter 2). Correct four more mistakes.

Writing Tip

When you write a complaint letter, clearly state the problem and ask for a solution.

1.
Kenneth Assam
35 Central Ave., Apt. 4D
Chicago, IL 60624

August 3, 2010

Pandora Chang
603 Washington St., Apt. 101
Chicago, IL 60625

Dear Ms. Chang:

I am writing to let you know that the faucet in my bathroom sink is broken again. The handle doesn't turn off all the way, and a lot of water is leaking. I think it's getting worse.

Could you please call a plumber to fix or replace the faucet? Or can we call a plumber and bill you? The lease says that it is your responsibility. It needs to be fixed soon because we are losing a lot of water. Please call me. Thank you.

Sincerely yours,
Kenneth Assam

2.
October 3, 2010

Dear Ms. Chang:

          am
I writing to let you know that my refrigerator is broken. It doesn't stay on all the time, so my food is going bad. I think it getting worse. It need to be fixed or replaced. My lease say that the landlord responsible for making sure that all appliances work. Please call me at (773) 888-1000. Thank you. I look forward to hearing from you very soon.

Sincerely yours,
Marina Levy
Marina Levy
Apt. 4E

A Complete the chart. Use the words in the box. Some words can go in both categories. Then add three more of your own words to each category.

Learning Strategy:
Organize Words

Organize your vocabulary into categories to help you learn and remember it.

> ~~bookshelf~~   coffee table   chair   microwave
> oven   refrigerator   sofa

kitchen	living room
	bookshelf

B Check the adjectives that can be used with each item.

	leaking	cracked	broken	burnt (out)	ripped
1. window		✓	✓		
2. bathtub					
3. carpet					
4. faucet					
5. microwave					
6. sink					
7. lightbulb					
8. curtains					
9. doorbell					
10. toilet					

A Complete the sentences. Circle the correct words.

1. Would you rather (buy)/ **to buy** from a private individual or from a dealer?

2. Daniel would prefer **drive** / **to drive** an automatic transmission.

3. We'd rather not **buy** / **to buy** a car without a warranty.

4. My wife would prefer a compact car **from** / **to** an SUV.

5. She says she'd rather get good gas mileage **than** / **to** have more space.

6. I'd prefer not **buy** / **to buy** a car with a lot of miles on it.

7. Many people would prefer not **drive** / **to drive** a large car.

8. We'd rather **look** / **looking** at some other cars before we make a decision.

B Complete the conversation. Use the expressions in the box.

> we'd prefer   we'd rather   we'd rather not
> ~~would you prefer~~   would you rather

A: We're interested in buying a used car.

B: What kind of car are you looking for? Do you want a large car? Or

(1.) ___would you prefer___ something small?

A: Well, we have four children, so I think (2.) _____ get a van. We don't want

an SUV. And (3.) _____ something that gets good mileage.

B: Do you want to pay cash, or (4.) _____ get financing? We can do either.

A: We'd like to pay cash, if that's possible. (5.) _____ get financing.

C Read the paragraph. Correct four more mistakes. Use *would rather* or *would prefer*. Use contractions if possible.

My wife and I are looking for a new car. There are a lot of options. I'd prefer ^to^ have a car that gets good gas mileage, even a hybrid if we can afford it. But my wife would prefer have a big car that has a lot of space. She rather have a van or an SUV, because they are more practical. Both of us are concerned about safety. We had prefer to have air bags than air-conditioning! And we agree that we rather buy from a dealer because a dealer would offer a warranty.

D MAKE IT PERSONAL. Look at the ads. Which car would you prefer? Write five sentences. Use *would rather (not)* or *would prefer (not)*. Explain your choices.

2009 four-door compact car, $7,000, 54,000 miles, silver, very reliable, runs great, only one owner, excellent gas mileage, save on gas! Private seller, call Tom (617) 555-2867.

2007 sport utility vehicle, $8,000, 107,000 miles, red, sunroof and CD player, front and side air bags, dealer financing available, one-year dealer warranty. Visit Greenville Used Car Dealership today!

I'd rather have the compact car because it gets good gas mileage.

1. _____

2. _____

3. _____

4. _____

5. _____

LIFE SKILLS

Complete the online insurance application. Use your own information. Make up details if necessary.

State Car Insurance

APPLICANT/ DRIVER

First name: _____ Last name: _____ Gender: ○ M ○ F

Date of birth: _____

Address: Street: _____ City: _____ State: _____ Zip: _____

Is vehicle located at this address? ○ yes ○ no

Telephone number: Day: _____ Evening: _____

Do you currently have auto insurance? ○ yes ○ no

Marital status: ○ single ○ married ○ divorced ○ widowed

Full-time student? ○ yes ○ no

How long have you been driving? _____ years

At what age did you obtain your U.S. driver's license? _____

VEHICLE INFORMATION

Year: _____ Make: _____ Model: _____

Year you bought the vehicle: _____

Hybrid vehicle? ○ yes ○ no

Safety features of the vehicle: ○ anti-lock brakes ○ front air bags ○ side air bags ○ anti-theft alarm

Is the vehicle used for business? ○ yes ○ no

How many days per week is the vehicle driven to work or school? _____

Estimated annual mileage: _____ miles

STUDY SKILL: Use a pie chart

A Look at the pie charts. Answer the questions.

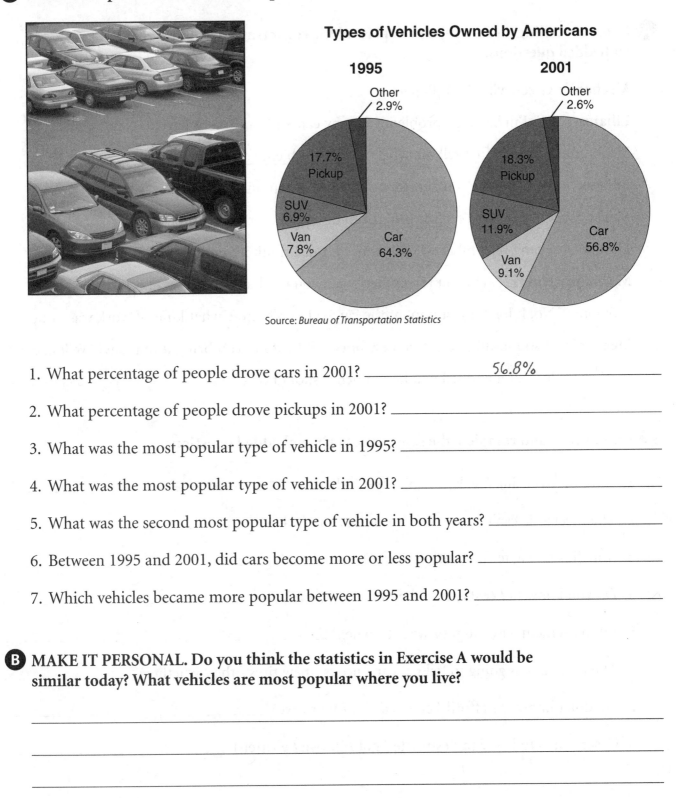

Types of Vehicles Owned by Americans

1995

Other 2.9%
17.7% Pickup
SUV 6.9%
Van 7.8%
Car 64.3%

2001

Other 2.6%
18.3% Pickup
SUV 11.9%
Van 9.1%
Car 56.8%

Source: *Bureau of Transportation Statistics*

1. What percentage of people drove cars in 2001? _____ *56.8%* _____

2. What percentage of people drove pickups in 2001? _____

3. What was the most popular type of vehicle in 1995? _____

4. What was the most popular type of vehicle in 2001? _____

5. What was the second most popular type of vehicle in both years? _____

6. Between 1995 and 2001, did cars become more or less popular? _____

7. Which vehicles became more popular between 1995 and 2001? _____

B MAKE IT PERSONAL. Do you think the statistics in Exercise A would be similar today? What vehicles are most popular where you live?

_____

_____

_____

_____

A Liliana is calling an auto repair shop. Read the conversation. Underline the embedded questions.

Mechanic: Greeneville Auto Repair.

Liliana: Hi. I'm having a problem with my car, and I think I'll have to bring it in.

Mechanic: All right, first tell me <u>what kind of problem you're having</u>.

Liliana: Well, my car is making a noise when I step on the brakes.

Mechanic: OK. Can you tell me if it's been doing this for a long time?

Liliana: I can't remember when it started. But I think it's getting worse.

Mechanic: Hmm . . . Do you remember when you last had the brakes checked?

Liliana: No, I don't. I just bought the car, so I don't know what kind of work was done.

Mechanic: It sounds like you need new brakes. Why don't you bring it in today? We'll take a

look at it and tell you how much it should cost.

B Unscramble and complete the sentences. Form embedded questions.

1. I wonder (causing / leak / is / oil / the / what) <u>what is causing the oil leak.</u>

2. The mechanic can't figure out (is / noise / the / what) _____

3. Min-Ji is trying to find out (car / if / is / her / ready) _____

4. Do you know (a / costs / how / much / new / radiator) _____

5. I don't remember (bought / we / it / when) _____

6. The mechanic is going to tell us (car / needs / new tires / the / whether) _____

7. We don't know (a / afford / can / car / if / new / we) _____

8. Cesar wants to know (a / estimate / got / if / we / written) _____

C Complete the conversation between a customer and a salesperson. Change
the customer's direct questions to embedded questions.

Binh: Hi. I wonder _____*if you can help me.*_____ I need some new tires.
(**1. Can you help me?**)

Salesperson: We can do that. Do you know _____
(**2. How many do you want?**)

Binh: I'm not sure. I don't know _____ or not. Could you take
(**3. Do I need to change all of the tires?**)

a look and tell me _____
(**4. What do you think?**)

Salesperson: Well, it looks like you need the front two tires, anyway. The back ones are OK. Do you

want to do it now?

Binh: Could you give me an idea of _____
(**5. How much will it cost?**)

Salesperson: Let's see . . . It would be seventy-five dollars per tire.

Binh: OK. That's fine. I can do it now. Can you tell me _____
(**6. How long will it take?**)

Salesperson: It should take about forty-five minutes.

D Look at the pictures at an auto repair shop. Report the questions that the
customers are asking. Write embedded questions.

1. Omar is wondering _____*what time he can pick up the truck.*_____

2. Mary wants to know _____

3. Patty is asking _____

4. Jin-Su is asking _____

READ

Read the article. Where did the author get the statistics about traffic accidents? _____

Negligent Driving Most Common Cause of Traffic Accidents

The next time you are in a car, take a look at the drivers around you. Note how many of them are talking on a cell phone or adjusting their stereo, DVD player, or GPS system. With so much going on inside our cars, it's no surprise that, according to a recent study by the National Highway and Transportation Safety Association (NHTSA), the largest single cause of motor vehicle accidents in the U.S. is drivers not paying attention to the road.

In over 21 percent of accidents, the cause was attributed to inadequate **surveillance**—that is, a situation in which a driver did not look for, or failed to see, a safety **hazard** in the road ahead. A further 14 percent of accidents were caused by **distractions** such as talking on a cell phone or with a passenger, eating and drinking, looking at scenery, and adjusting stereo or vehicle controls. Driver inattention, such as daydreaming, accounted for 4 percent of accidents.

According to the NHTSA study, many accidents are also caused by drivers making poor decisions. Over 13 percent of accidents were attributed to drivers going too fast for weather or road conditions. Another 8 percent of accidents resulted from the driver misjudging other drivers' actions or speed. Aggressive driving, such as driving too close to the car in front of you (tailgating), frequently changing lanes, and refusing to **yield** to other vehicles, caused 2 percent of accidents.

In the past several years, engineers have introduced crash-avoidance technology to help prevent accidents. For example, some cars have dashboard warning systems that can alert you to danger. Distance monitors judge the distance between your car and the vehicle in front of you. Lane monitors alert you when your car is drifting out of its lane. Blind spot **sensors** let you know when another car is nearby but not visible in your mirrors. However, the **implications** of the NHTSA study are clear: Drivers themselves can prevent the majority of deaths and injuries that occur on our roads every year by being more alert.

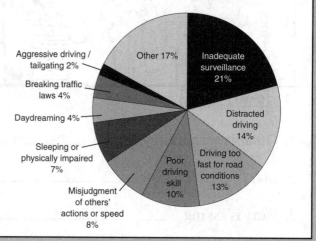

Accident Causes

- Aggressive driving / tailgating 2%
- Breaking traffic laws 4%
- Daydreaming 4%
- Sleeping or physically impaired 7%
- Misjudgment of others' actions or speed 8%
- Other 17%
- Inadequate surveillance 21%
- Distracted driving 14%
- Driving too fast for road conditions 13%
- Poor driving skill 10%

Source: www.nhtsa.gov

CHECK YOUR UNDERSTANDING

Reading Skill:
Use Visuals

Use charts, graphs, and other visuals
to learn important facts.

A Read the article again. Circle the statistics in the pie
chart that are mentioned in the article.

B Complete the sentences about the article.

1. More than 21 percent of accidents were caused by _____.

2. Examples of common driving _____ include talking on a cell phone and

   adjusting stereo controls.

3. _____ percent of accidents were attributed to drivers going too fast

   for conditions.

4. Driving too close to the car in front of you is called _____.

5. Refusing to yield to other vehicles is an example of _____.

6. Three examples of crash-avoidance technology are _____,

   _____, and _____.

C WORD WORK. Find the boldface words in the article. Match the words
with the definitions.

1. ____ **surveillance**   a. equipment used to sense sound, movement, light, etc.

2. ____ **hazard**   b. something that is not directly said but that is suggested

3. ____ **distraction**   c. to allow other cars, people, etc., to go first

4. ____ **yield**   d. the act of watching something carefully

5. ____ **sensor**   e. something that takes attention away from what you are doing

6. ____ **implication**   f. something that may be dangerous or cause accidents

A Read the sentences. Underline the verbs. Mark the earlier action *1* and the later action *2*.

1. The road <u>was</u> slippery because it <u>had rained</u> the night before.
   > (2 above "was", 1 above "had rained")

2. The family had just left home when the accident happened.

3. The driver said that he hadn't seen the cyclist.

4. Jackie had heard about the accident on the radio, so she decided to take a different route.

5. I got a ticket because my registration had expired.

6. Carlo ran out of gas. He had forgotten to fill up the tank again!

B Complete the sentences. Use the past perfect.

1. Main Street was closed this afternoon. There _____*had been*_____ a bad accident there in
   (be)
   the morning. A driver _____ control of his car and crashed into a tree.
   (lose)

2. I _____ to change lanes when I heard a loud honk. There was a car in the
   (start)
   other lane already, but I didn't see it. I _____ my side and rearview
   (check)
   mirrors before moving into the lane, but I _____ my blind spot.
   (not check)

3. Jane and Steve _____ just _____ out of the supermarket
   (step)
   when they saw a tow truck towing their car away. They _____ in a fire lane
   (park)
   by mistake.

4. Sam had a fender bender yesterday. I was surprised, because he is a very safe driver. Until
   yesterday, he _____ never _____ an accident. He
   (have)
   _____ never even _____ a traffic ticket!
   (get)

C Complete the paragraph. Use the simple past or past perfect.

We ___had just gotten___ into the car when we _____ a loud crash. We
      (1. just get)   **(2. hear)**

_____ across the street and _____ that a car
   (3. look)   **(4. see)**

_____ into a streetlight! We _____ over to see if the driver
   (5. crash)   **(6. run)**

was all right. The driver _____ that a cat _____ right in
                         (7. explain)   **(8. run)**

front of the car. He tried to avoid it and lost control of the car. The driver

_____ hurt, but he _____ very upset because he
   (9. not be)   **(10. be)**

_____ in an accident before. He _____ also very worried
  (11. never be)   **(12. be)**

about his car. He _____ it the week before!
           (13. only buy)

D Look at the timelines. Write one sentence about each timeline. Use the past perfect and the word in parentheses.

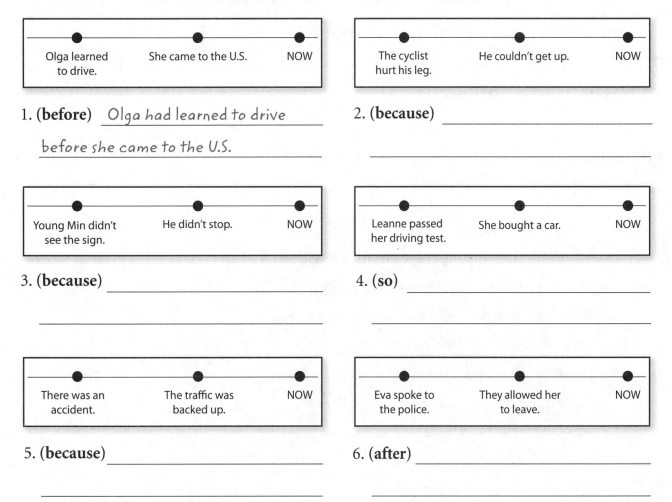

Olga learned to drive. — She came to the U.S. — NOW

The cyclist hurt his leg. — He couldn't get up. — NOW

1. **(before)** _Olga had learned to drive before she came to the U.S._

2. **(because)** _____

Young Min didn't see the sign. — He didn't stop. — NOW

Leanne passed her driving test. — She bought a car. — NOW

3. **(because)** _____

4. **(so)** _____

There was an accident. — The traffic was backed up. — NOW

Eva spoke to the police. — They allowed her to leave. — NOW

5. **(because)** _____

6. **(after)** _____

A Complete the paragraph. Use the time words in the box.

> After   Finally   First   then   Then

> **Writing Tip**
>
> Use time words and phrases to signal the steps in a process.

Joe and Elaine decided that they needed a minivan for their growing family. (1.) _____, they did some research to find which kinds of minivans had good safety records and good gas mileage. (2.) _____ they found a model that they both liked. They worked out how much it should cost, and (3.) _____ they went to a dealership to talk to a salesperson. (4.) _____ talking to the salesperson, Joe and Elaine decided to buy one of the minivans they looked at. They completed the paperwork and drove their new minivan home. (5.) _____, they went to put it in the garage. But the minivan didn't fit. It was too high. They had forgotten to measure the space!

B Read the paragraph. Correct five more mistakes.

> First, I spoke to my cousin Dimitri. He is an auto
> mechanic, and he sometimes ~~have~~ has cars for sale. He told
> me that he can help me find a good car that got good
> mileage. After that, my family and I discussed how much
> could we pay. We didn't have enough money, so I go to
> the bank to find out whether could I get a loan. I filled
> out some forms, and get a loan for $5,000. Then my
> cousin and I started looking at used cars on the Internet.

A Label the picture. Use the words in the box.

bumper	fender	headlight
hood	radiator	rearview mirror
side mirror	~~sunroof~~	tire
turn signal light	windshield wipers	windshield

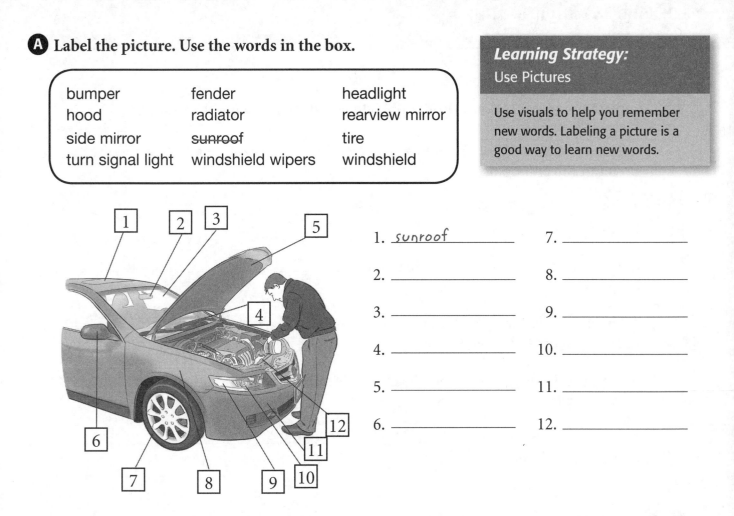

1. _sunroof_   7. _____

2. _____   8. _____

3. _____   9. _____

4. _____   10. _____

5. _____   11. _____

6. _____   12. _____

B Circle the word that is different in each list. Explain your answer.

1. (headlight,) pickup, minivan, SUV _Headlight is different because it's not a type of car._

2. CD player, sunroof, power steering, tires _____

3. seat belt, air bag, hood, antilock brakes _____

4. premium, deductible, bumper, policy _____

5. brakes, coolant, transmission fluid, gas _____

6. driver's license, turn signal, vehicle registration, insurance card _____

7. compact, four-door, reliable, estimate _____

Lessons 1 & 2: Grammar

A Complete the conversations. Unscramble the words to make questions.

1. **A:** (long / waiting / how / been / you / have) <u>How long have you been waiting?</u>
   B: About fifteen minutes.

2. **A:** (tired / recently / been / has / feeling / she) _____
   B: Yes, she has.

3. **A:** (you / doing / lately / been / what / have) _____
   B: I've been very busy at work.

4. **A:** (hurting / has / leg / his / been / only at night) _____
   B: No, sometimes during the day, too.

5. **A:** (in / you / feeling / any / back / pain / have / your / been) _____
   B: No, I haven't.

6. **A:** (has / medication / what / been / Mrs. Lee / taking) _____
   B: Just a pain reliever.

B Complete the conversation. Use the present perfect continuous.

Leann: Dr. Park, I'm worried about Alissa. She <u>hasn't been feeling</u> well for several days.
         (1. not / feel)
She _____ a lot and _____ her stomach.
      (2. cry)   **(3. hold)**

Dr. Park: _____ all the time or only after eating?
      (4. it / happen)

Leann: It's usually after she eats and then it calms down.

Dr. Park: Hmm. _____ OK?
         (5. she / sleep)

Leann: Yes, I think so. She _____ up
            (6. not / wake)
during the night.

Dr. Park: That's good. I think she'll be fine, but we should

do some tests.

C Rewrite the sentences. Use the present perfect continuous with *for* or *since*. More than one answer may be possible.

1. Olga started taking heart medication two years ago, and she still takes it.

   Olga has been taking heart medication for two years.

2. I started eating healthier food last month. I still eat healthy food.

   _____

3. We arrived at the doctor's office an hour ago, and we're still waiting.

   _____

4. Tranh didn't feel well last night, and he still doesn't feel well.

   _____

5. The children aren't sleeping well. It started a few weeks ago.

   _____

6. My grandfather started taking insulin last year. He still takes it.

   _____

D Read the e-mail. Correct five more mistakes.

Dear Juliana,

    How are you? Have you been ~~feel~~ *feeling* better lately? I hope so! Things are fine here. Frank

hasn't working so hard, so that's good. Both of the kids have bad colds. Katie haven't

been feeling well enough to go to school, but Leo has been go to school. I've be staying

home from work with the kids, but I'll go back as soon as Katie is better.

    How are you? What you have been doing? Write when you have a minute and let me

know how things are going.

Xiao-Yan

LIFE SKILLS

A Read the health insurance form. How many family members does Rafael want covered (including himself)? _____

Bell Services Company

Health Insurance Enrollment Form

Enrollment Period: You must enroll in your health insurance plan within 60 days of being hired. You can only make changes during the first two weeks of January and the first two weeks of June.

Section 1: Employee Information

Name: _Rafael Lorca_

SS#: _123-45-6789_

Address: _4839 West 7th Street_

City: _Oakland_   State: _CA_   Zip: _94601_

Phone number: _510-555-8910_

Birth date: _08/12/1978_

Marital status: ☐ Single   ☑ Married   ☐ Divorced

Gender: ☑ Male   ☐ Female

Date of hire: _August 3, 2009_   Type of employment: ☑ Full-time   ☐ Part-time

Section 2: Enrollment and Coverage

☑ Enroll

☐ Change (I want a different plan.)

☐ Waive (I do not wish to enroll in the plan.)

Coverage:

☐ Medical only

☑ Medical and Dental

Section 3: Family Members Covered

(check all that apply)

☑ Self   ☑ Spouse   ☑ Dependent(s)

	Name	Birth date
Spouse	_Carolina Lorca_	_12/23/1981_
Dependent	_Robert Lorca_	_2/14/2006_
Dependent		
Dependent		

B Look at the form again. Read the statements. Circle *True* or *False*.

1. Rafael started working for Bell Services on August 3, 2009.	**True**	**False**
2. Rafael works full-time at the company.	**True**	**False**
3. It's possible not to accept the insurance plan.	**True**	**False**
4. Rafael doesn't want his wife enrolled in the plan.	**True**	**False**
5. Rafael has two dependent children.	**True**	**False**

DICTIONARY SKILL: Identify parts of speech

A Read the dictionary entries. Circle the part of each entry that identifies the part of speech. Underline the part that gives a synonym (a word with the same meaning).

im•mu•nize /ˈɪmyəˌnaɪz/ *v.* [T] to protect someone from disease by giving him/her a vaccine ⓈⓎⓃ inoculate, vaccinate: *Have you been **immunized against** tuberculosis?*

1.

med•i•cine /ˈmɛdəsən/ *n.* **1** [CU] a substance used for treating illness: *Remember to **take** your **medicine**.* | *Medicines should be kept away from children.*

2.

in•oc•u•late /ɪˈnakyəˌleɪt/ *v.* [T] (formal) to protect someone against a disease by introducing a weak form of it into his/her body ⓈⓎⓃ immunize, vaccinate: *Children should be **inoculated against** measles.*

3.

vac•ci•nate /ˈvæksəˌneɪt/ *v.* [T] to protect someone from a disease by giving him/her a vaccine ⓈⓎⓃ immunize, inoculate: *Have you been **vaccinated against** measles?*

4.

Source: *Longman Dictionary of American English*

B Answer the questions about the dictionary entries in Exercise A.

1. Which three words are synonyms? _____

2. Which word is a noun? _____

3. Which words are verbs? _____

4. Which words use the preposition *against*? _____

5. Which word is commonly used with the verb *take*? _____

A Complete the sentences. Match the sentence parts.

1. __f__ I cut my hand last weekend. It was bleeding so heavily

2. ____ Then, he was driving so fast

3. ____ When we got to the emergency room, there was such a long line

4. ____ The nurse was so worried about my hand

5. ____ I saw a doctor who was so good

6. ____ When we finally got home, we were so tired

a. that I thought we might have an accident.

b. that he put me first in line.

c. that I didn't feel any pain when she put the stitches in.

d. that we just wanted to go to bed.

e. that we didn't know if I'd be able to see a doctor.

f. that my husband decided to take me to the emergency room.

B Complete the conversations. Use *so* or *such*.

1. **A:** I'm worried about my grandmother. She has ___such___ bad headaches sometimes that she can't get out of bed.

   B: That's terrible. Has she seen a doctor?

   A: Well, she's _____ scared of doctors and hospitals that she doesn't want to.

2. **A:** Louisa fell off her bike yesterday and cut her head. It was bleeding _____ badly! I was _____ scared that I was shaking.

   B: Oh no! What did you do?

   A: I called 911 and they came _____ quickly that I couldn't believe it. They stopped the bleeding and calmed both of us down. They did _____ a good job!

3. **A:** My doctor told me that my lifestyle and diet is _____ bad that I might have health problems if I don't change.

   B: What are you going to do?

   A: I'm trying to learn about nutrition, but there's _____ a lot to learn! And, it's _____ hard to change habits.

C Look at the picture. Read the patient's reasons for not living a healthier life. Combine the sentences with *so . . . that* or *such . . . that*.

1. I'm busy. I have to eat fast food.

   I am so busy that I have to eat fast food.

2. I work long hours. I don't have time to exercise.

   _____

3. It takes a long time to get to the gym. I don't go. _____

4. Walking is boring. I don't do it. _____

5. I'm really bad at cooking. I don't want to try it. _____

6. Fresh vegetables are expensive. I can't afford to buy them. _____

7. I'm really tired after work. I just want to watch TV. _____

D Write five sentences with *so . . . that* and *such . . . that*. Use the ideas in the chart and your own ideas.

Health insurance	so	expensive	can't afford it
My doctor	such	a busy office	hard to get an appointment
I'm		tired	don't want to go out tonight
My sister		a healthy person	she never eats fast food

Health insurance is so expensive that many people
can't afford it.

1. _____

2. _____

3. _____

4. _____

5. _____

READ

Read the article. How much exercise do you need for general health? _____

EXERCISE: The Key to a Healthy Life

Want to know the secret to living a long, healthy life? Get physically fit. There is no **substitute**! Physical exercise provides health benefits that cannot be obtained in any other way.

You don't need to be a serious athlete to have a healthy level of activity. Just scheduling thirty minutes of activity a day, such as walking, bicycling, climbing steps, or working in the garden, can make a big difference.

Studies show that regular exercise could **prolong** your life. In one study of a group of retired men, the men who did little or no activity had a death rate twice as high as that of men who walked two or more miles daily. Over a twelve-year period, 40 percent of the non-exercisers died compared to 20 percent in the exercise group. There are also studies that show a **reduction** in the risk of certain cancers, including breast and colon cancers.

How much exercise do you need?

- For general health, the goal is a total of thirty minutes of exercise most days of the week. Three ten-minute walks are as good as one thirty-minute walk.

- For weight loss, you need about forty-five minutes of moderate activity every day.

- On days when you don't have time to meet these goals, do as much as you can. Even ten minutes of exercise is better than none at all.

Exercise and health
- Do you want to lose weight? Exercise is **crucial** for maintaining weight.
- Do you need to stop smoking? Exercise makes it easier and increases your chance of success.
- Is your blood pressure or cholesterol high? Exercise helps control both.

Check with your doctor
Before starting any exercise plan, talk with your doctor if:
- you are a male over forty-five or a female over fifty years old
- you have had a heart attack or some heart trouble
- you have diabetes or high blood pressure
- you have bone or **joint** problems that may be affected by exercise

CHECK YOUR UNDERSTANDING

Reading Skill:

Scanning a List for Details

Read information in a bulleted list quickly to look for details such as facts and numbers.

A Look at the bulleted information in the article. Answer the questions.

1. How much exercise is necessary for weight loss?

_____

2. What three health goals will exercise help support?

_____

3. At what age should males talk to their doctor before starting an exercise program?

_____

4. At what age should females talk to their doctor before starting an exercise program?

_____

5. If you have high blood pressure, what should you do before starting an exercise plan?

_____

B MAKE IT PERSONAL. What do you think are the most important benefits of exercise?

_____

_____

C WORD WORK. Find the boldface words in the article. Match the words with the definitions.

1. ____ **substitute**   a. extremely important

2. ____ **prolong**   b. a part of the body where two bones meet

3. ____ **reduction**   c. something you use instead of something else

4. ____ **crucial**   d. to make something last longer

5. ____ **joint**   e. a decrease

A Read the school memo. Underline two more examples of advice or suggestions with *should*. Circle three examples of requirements with *must*.

MEMO .

To: All Parents
From: Judith Chung, Principal

Subject: Health and wellness for students

We are implementing some new health and wellness strategies this year. Studies show that <u>students should be getting more exercise during the school day</u> and that exercise can actually help learning. Here are some new programs:

- The gym will be open for an hour before school and an hour after school. Several teachers have volunteered to supervise. Students must wear athletic shoes or they will not be allowed into the gym.

- We are offering exercise classes for the whole family on the first Saturday of every month. These are free, but you should register in advance. Classes fill up fast.

- Good nutrition is a part of health, too. We all should aim for at least five servings of fruit and vegetables daily. The cafeteria will be offering healthful options to help with this. Please encourage your child to choose these healthful options.

And, finally, a reminder that student health forms must be completed and handed in by September 8. Also, parents of new students must fill out a Family Data form by September 14.

B Complete the conversation. Circle the correct words.

A: We got a notice from Lucia's school today. It says that all students (must) / **should** have a physical examination before the first day of school. And all immunizations **ought to** / **must** be up to date. It's a state law.

B: They really **should / should not** send these notices earlier in the summer.

A: I know. The clinic gets pretty busy just before school starts. It's hard to get an appointment.

B: Must / Should I call the clinic next week and make an appointment?

A: Yes, you **had better not / should**. Actually, you **had better / must** call right now. We don't want to wait until the last minute.

C Complete the conversations. Use the words in parentheses and *should*, *ought to*, or *had better*. More than one answer may be possible.

1. **A:** I get sick every winter. Last year I was out sick for two weeks. I hate it.

   B: (flu shot) *You should get a flu shot.*

2. **A:** I have had an earache for weeks and I'm having trouble hearing.

   B: (go to the doctor) _____

3. **A:** I need to eat more healthful food, but I don't know how to cook.

   B: (take a cooking class) _____

4. **A:** My family never gets any exercise.

   B: (go for walks together) _____

5. **A:** I'm working really hard and feel totally stressed out.

   B: (take some time off) _____

D Look at the pictures. How can the people stay healthy? On notepaper, write advice. Use *should*, *shouldn't*, *ought to*, *had better*, and *had better not*.

A Read the paragraph comparing the health care systems in South Korea and the United States. Write a title that shows the main idea of the paragraph.

_____

Health care in Korea is a lot different from health care in the U.S. First, it's more expensive in the U.S. than in Korea, even with insurance. When you have insurance in Korea, it covers everything, including the dentist and eye doctor. I was surprised when I came to the U.S. and found that my insurance only covered medical doctors. I was also surprised to find that you have to pay a copay when you go to the doctor, even with insurance. We don't have this in Korea. Once I had to go to the emergency room here and I couldn't believe how long I had to wait. There were a lot of people waiting. In Korea, we only go to the ER for a real emergency, but people here go for almost anything.

B Read the paragraph. Correct five more mistakes.

The health care systems in Switzerland and the U.S. ~~is~~ _are_ fairly similar. In both, you buys private insurance, and there are different packages to choose from. And in both countries there is a lot of problems because the cost is such high. One big difference is that in the U.S. you often get insurance from your employer, but in Switzerland, you doesn't. Also, I was surprised to learn that there is dental insurance in the U.S. In Switzerland, we don't has dental insurance. We have to pay for visits to the dentist.

A Choose five new vocabulary words that you learned in this unit. Write each word. Then use the word in a sentence.

side effect: Many medications can cause side effects, such as dizziness or nausea.

1. _____

2. _____

3. _____

4. _____

5. _____

B Complete the sentences. Circle the correct word.

1. My grandfather has been feeling very (tired)/ **tiredness** lately, so he's going to see the doctor.

2. One possible side effect of this medication is **dizzy / dizziness**, so be careful when you take it.

3. **Obese / Obesity** is becoming such a problem in the U.S. that it's a national epidemic.

4. My aunt is **diabetic / diabetes**, so she has to watch her diet carefully.

5. Don't drive a car after taking this medicine because it can make you **sleepy / sleepiness**.

6. If your arms and legs feel **numb / numbness**, call your doctor immediately.

7. I called 911 when my grandmother was so **weak / weakness** that she couldn't walk.

8. Ling is so **allergic / allergy** to peanuts that she could stop breathing if she eats one.

Lessons 1 & 2: Grammar

A Read the introduction to the Greenville Elementary School Parents' Guide. Draw one line under the adverb clauses of reason. Draw two lines under the adverb clauses and infinitives of purpose.

> ### Greenville Elementary School
> ### Parents' Guide
>
> Welcome to our school! As a parent, you are welcome on campus <u>because you are an important part of your child's education.</u> There are many things that you can do to help your child succeed in school. First, make sure that your child gets enough sleep, since well-rested children perform better in school. In the morning, make sure that your child has a good breakfast so that he or she is ready to learn. Since children do not always tell you what is happening in school, make sure you check homework, ask questions, and stay in touch with your child's teacher. Finally, read the school bulletins to find out how you can volunteer at school. Parents are an important part of the Greenville Team!

B Complete the sentences. Match the sentence parts.

1. __c__ It's good to have a school near your home because

2. ____ Children should get to school on time so that

3. ____ Schools hold parent-teacher meetings to

4. ____ After-school programs are popular because

5. ____ The class went to the museum to

6. ____ The school secretary called Grace's parents to

a. find out why she was absent.

b. inform parents about their children's progress.

c. your children can get to school on time.

d. many parents are working full-time.

e. see an art exhibition.

f. they don't miss the beginning of class.

C Complete the conversations from a parent-teacher conference. Use *because, since, so that,* or *to.*

1. **Mrs. Torres:** Why are the children sitting together at desks?

   Teacher: We do it ___so that___ the children can interact with each other. They work in groups, _____ research shows that children learn better that way.

2. **Mr. Brandon:** How are the children learning science?

   Teacher: Well, we have a garden _____ students can learn about plants, and we take students to the science museum _____ do hands-on experiments.

3. **Mrs. Cervantes:** Tell me about your after-school program.

   Teacher: The children are grouped by grade levels _____ work together on homework. Tutoring is available _____ some children need extra help. The students also have free time outdoors _____ they get some exercise.

D Combine the sentences. Use *because, since, so that,* or *to.* More than one answer may be possible.

1. We wanted to speak to you. Alex is having some trouble in school.

   We wanted to speak to you because Alex is having some trouble in school.

2. We are meeting with Mi-Young's guidance counselor. We'll discuss her college plans.

   _____

3. We'd like you to attend our Parents as Partners event. You'll learn our goals for the year.

   _____

4. My son gets into trouble at school. He is bored with his schoolwork.

   _____

5. My son doesn't know anyone at his new school. We encouraged him to join some after-school clubs.

   _____

LIFE SKILLS

A Read Ariana's elementary school report card. How many times a year does she receive a report card? _____

GREENVILLE SCHOOL DISTRICT REPORT CARD

Name: Ariana Li   School: Greenville Elementary School
Teacher: Ms. Rose Kirkham   Grade: 4

Key:
4   Demonstrating high achievement of requirements
3   Meeting requirements consistently
2   Developing the skills and understanding needed to meet requirements
1   Needing significant improvement to meet requirements

Grading Periods

LANGUAGE ARTS	1st	2nd	3rd	4th
Reads aloud with fluency and accuracy	3			
Understands main events in a story	3			
Knows how to use a dictionary	3			
Writes compositions	2			
Uses correct punctuation	3			
Writes summaries of main ideas	2			

MATHEMATICS	1st	2nd	3rd	4th
Counts whole numbers to 1,000,000	4			
Adds and subtracts numbers of three or more digits	3			
Multiplies and divides two-digit numbers	2			
Identifies different geometric shapes (such as triangles, squares, rectangles)	3			

WORK HABITS / SOCIAL SKILLS	1st	2nd	3rd	4th
Works well with other children	3			
Follows directions	3			
Accepts responsibility	3			
Completes homework	3			

TEACHER'S COMMENTS
Ariana is a good worker and a pleasure to have in class. She has made good progress in mathematics this semester, and her reading has improved, too. Keep up the reading at home! She still needs to work on writing. She is not meeting requirements in that area. I recommend extra tutoring after school. I would also like her to talk more in class. We need to encourage her to overcome her shyness.

B **Complete the statements about Ariana's report card.**

1. Ariana is in the _____ grade.

2. Ariana is demonstrating high achievement in _____.

3. In language arts, Ariana is not meeting requirements with _____.

4. In mathematics, Ariana has trouble with _____.

5. Ariana's teacher recommends that she get _____ after school.

6. Ariana's teacher would like her to _____ in class.

STUDY SKILL: Use a bar graph

Look at the bar graphs. Answer the questions.

Parent involvement in child's school, 1996–2003

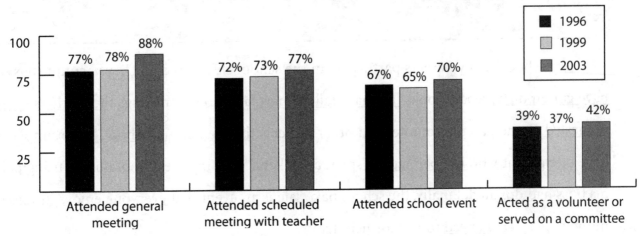

Source: U.S. Department of Education

1. What are the two most popular ways for parents to be involved in their child's school?

_____

2. What is the least popular way for parents to be involved in their child's school?

_____

3. What percentage of parents attended a general meeting in 1996? _____

4. What percentage of parents attended a school event in 2003? _____

5. Is parent participation in school increasing or decreasing? _____

A Read the paragraph. Look at the underlined adjective clauses. Circle the person or thing that each adjective clause gives information about.

At our school, many parents participate in the school clean-up day. They vacuum (rugs) that have gotten dirty, repair books that have fallen apart, and do other things the teachers have requested. Some parents volunteer on other projects that benefit the school. For example, we have one parent who is a painter. He spent a weekend painting the school library using paint his boss had donated. Finally, the school bake sale is an event that everyone enjoys. It raises money the teachers need to pay for field trips.

B Complete the sentences. Match the sentence parts.

1. __d__ My children go to the same school

2. _____ The walls are covered with pictures

3. _____ There is an auditorium

4. _____ Many of the children come from families

5. _____ There are volunteer tutors

a. who help children with their homework.

b. that immigrated to the U.S.

c. the children have painted.

d. that I went to.

e. that students use for concerts and performances.

C Complete the sentences. Circle the correct words.

1. Julian was working on a project **who** / **(that)** took the whole weekend.

2. At bake sales, children sell cakes and cookies **that** / **who** their parents have made.

3. The child that **read** / **reads** the most books over the summer will win a prize.

4. Many parents are looking for schools **which** / **who** have after-school programs.

5. After-school care is important for parents who **is** / **are** working full time.

6. It's important to have a principal **which** / **who** communicates well with parents.

7. The school district gave an award to the school **that** / **who** had the highest test scores.

D Combine the sentences. Use *who, that, which,* or *no pronoun.* More than one correct answer may be possible.

1. We enrolled Sun-Young in a school. The school had good test scores.

   We enrolled Sun-Young in a school that had good test scores.

2. Sue had a teacher. She liked the teacher.

   _____

3. The teachers meet in a room. The room is used for conferences.

   _____

4. Luis couldn't do the homework. The teacher had assigned the homework.

   _____

5. There is a special program for the children. The children get good grades.

   _____

6. Carmen takes a bus. The bus stops directly in front of her school.

   _____

READ

Read the letter to the editor. Answer the questions.

1. Why was the letter written?_____

_____

2. What will the school budget pay for?_____

_____

Letters to the Editor

Vote "Yes" for School Budget

As a teacher in the Greenville School District, I urge readers to vote for the school budget, which will provide **additional** funding for our district's public schools.

At a time when our district has been **adversely** affected by state budget cuts, this money is desperately needed for a variety of reasons. First, it will enable us to keep class sizes low. When class sizes are large, teachers have less time available to work with individual students. This measure would also provide funding for support staff, who help keep our schools clean and safe.

The new budget will also guarantee funds for art, music education, and librarians. Experts agree on the value of the arts, because research shows that children who take art and music classes perform better in school than those who do not. Currently, our school has an art room that is never used because we do not have an art teacher. We have a librarian who comes to our school only one day a week. Without more funding, next year we may have to reduce or **eliminate** our music program. This will affect the education of all of our students.

Finally, the budget provides for an increase in teachers' salaries, which have remained at the same level for five years. As a teacher, I find it demoralizing and **disheartening** to watch the cost of living rise every year without a corresponding rise in our pay. Many of us are spending our own money to pay for classroom supplies such as pens and copy paper. Teachers are already underpaid enough without having to take on this extra burden.

If we value our public schools, educational funding must be our state's highest priority. Please vote "Yes" to support our schools.

Joseph Cezus
English teacher
Greenville Elementary School

CHECK YOUR UNDERSTANDING

A Read the letter again. Complete the sentences, according to the letter.

1. Class sizes should be low because _____.

2. Support staff are important because _____.

3. Arts education is important because _____.

4. The art room and the library are not used more because _____.

5. Teachers need a salary increase because _____.

B Read the statements from the letter. Which are facts? Which are opinions? Write *Fact* or *Opinion*.

> **Reading Skill:**
> Distinguishing Fact from Opinion
>
> When you read, be careful to distinguish between facts and opinions.

1. _____ Research shows that children who take art and music classes perform better in school.

2. _____ Teachers' salaries have remained at the same level for five years.

3. _____ Many of us are spending our own money to pay for classroom supplies.

4. _____ Teachers are already underpaid enough without having to take on this extra burden.

5. _____ Educational funding must be our state's highest priority.

C WORD WORK. Find the boldface words in the article. Match the words with the definitions.

1. ____ **additional**   a. get rid of, cut

2. ____ **adversely**   b. negatively, in a bad way

3. ____ **eliminate**   c. more

4. ____ **disheartening**   d. disappointing, making you lose hope

A **Complete the conversations. Choose the correct words.**

1. **A:** What's wrong with that little boy under the slide? He's crying.

   B: He **must have** / **should** have fallen off.

   A: Where's his teacher?

   B: She's in the classroom. She **must not have** / **shouldn't have** seen it.

2. **A:** Luisa hit Shaheen, but the principal punished Shaheen. It wasn't his fault!

   B: The principal **must not have** / **shouldn't have** done that. He **must have** / **should have** punished Luisa instead.

3. **A:** Why is that girl staying in the classroom instead of going out to play?

   B: I don't know. She **might have** / **should have** done something wrong. Or she **might not have** / **must not have** finished her homework.

B **Complete the sentences. Use the expressions in the box. More than one answer may be possible.**

> could have   couldn't have   might have
>
> must have   should have   ~~shouldn't have~~

1. Diana, you have to miss recess. You ___*shouldn't have*___ thrown that paper airplane.

2. Sam went to the doctor yesterday. He _____ been sick.

3. You have not done your work. You _____ finished your paper by now.

4. Mr. Stevens's class isn't at lunch. The teacher _____ kept them late. Or they _____ gone on a field trip.

5. Felix has been absent all week, so he _____ known about the test today.

C Look at the pictures. What do you think happened? Write a sentence for each picture. Use the words in the box.

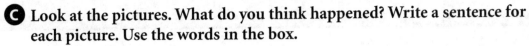

| may (not) have | might (not) have | could (not) have | must (not) have |

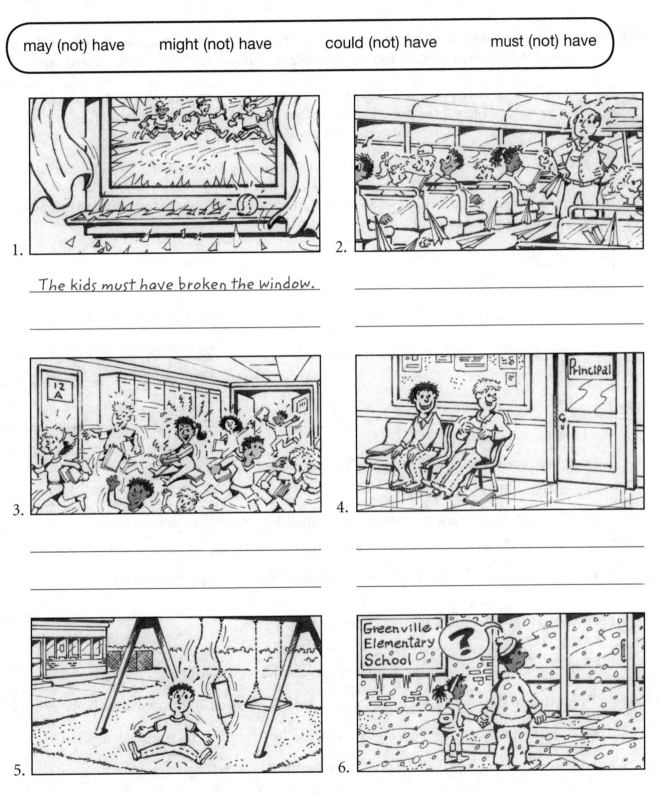

1.

The kids must have broken the window.

2.

3.

4.

5.

6.

A Look at the organization of a letter from a parent to a school principal. Then read the sentences. Decide which paragraph each sentence belongs with. Write the number.

As a parent of a child in Springfield Middle School, I was very upset to hear that the school board has decided to cut the popular after-school sports program next semester. ① Sports are beneficial to teenagers in many ways.

② I think there are many ways that we could raise money for after-school sports.

Sports should not be considered an "extra" at our school. Let's work together to keep this valuable program alive.

Sincerely,

Guillermo Villas

1. Exercise keeps teenagers healthy and physically fit. ___1___

2. One possibility would be to hold fund-raisers, such as a bake sales. _____

3. Success in sports helps children develop confidence and social skills. _____

4. Another option is to ask parents to pay a small fee or to volunteer. _____

5. Studies also show that teens who are involved in sports are less likely to use drugs. _____

6. Finally, we could ask local businesses to donate money or sponsor a team. _____

Writing Tip

When a writer uses more than one paragraph, it's important to put similar information together.

B Read the paragraph. Add a final "s" to five more words.

We would like to encourage all parent*s* to attend our monthly PTA meetings. The PTA helps to raise funds for many program and activities, and provide money for classroom materials. The PTA also organize volunteers to help at the talent show and other community event. Most importantly, PTA meetings keep parent informed about what's happening at school.

A Complete the sentences. Use the noun form of the underlined words. Use a dictionary if necessary.

Learning Strategy:
Making Nouns from Verbs

Many nouns are formed by adding endings such as *-ment* or *-ion*. Expand your vocabulary by learning the noun forms of verbs.

1. When Luisa <u>enrolled</u> in a computer class, she filled

   out an <u>enrollment</u> form.

2. The teacher said that Hae-Jin's math had <u>improved</u>.

   She was pleased with her _____.

3. It's important for parents to <u>participate</u> in their children's education. Parent _____

   helps children succeed in school.

4. More volunteers are needed to help <u>supervise</u> students during the after-school program.

   The parents are worried that there is not enough _____.

5. The teacher <u>assigns</u> a four-page paper every weekend. She says it's a difficult _____.

B Complete the sentences. Use the words in the box.

> conference   grades   open house   ~~report card~~   subject

1. Teachers complete a _____*report card*_____ for each student at the end of each semester.

   The students receive _____ from A to D for their work.

2. If a student is having problems at school, the teacher may ask to have a parent-teacher

   _____.

3. Many schools have an _____ where parents can meet the teachers and see

   examples of student work.

4. In high school, students have a different teacher for each _____. For

   example, a math teacher teaches math.

A Read the paragraph. Underline four more examples of *make / have / let / get* + verb.

> My company recently implemented some new policies. The general manager <u>made</u> all supervisors <u>take</u> a workplace safety class. After we took the class, the general manager had us review safety practices with all our workers. Reviewing safety is always helpful, especially because it gets you to discuss why safety is important. One problem I'd had was that my workers often didn't wear all their safety equipment. However, after they were reminded why the equipment is important, it was easier to get them to wear it. I told them if we went one month with everyone wearing all safety equipment all the time, I would let everyone take an extra break for a week. We'll see what happens.

B Complete the paragraph. Write the correct form of *make, have,* or *let*. More than one answer may be possible.

> Yesterday was my first day at my new job. First, my supervisor (1.) _____let_____ me have about twenty minutes to review the procedures in the training manual. Then she (2.) _____ me take the test for new employees. After that, she (3.) _____ me watch the other clerk complete some transactions. She (4.) _____ the other clerk to tell me about some of the problems he had when he started working there. That was really helpful! The supervisor (5.) _____ me practice transactions and then told me to take a break. I wanted to skip the break and keep working, but she (6.) _____ me take the break. That was good because I was tired!

C Look at the pictures. Write a sentence about what each manager says. Use the correct form of *make, have, let,* or *get.* More than one answer may be possible.

1. Jackie
   Could you possibly rush our order?
   Great, thanks very much.

   Jackie got the supplier to rush the order.

2. Jackie — Sufia — Bao
   Please help the new employees today.
   OK.
   Sure.

3. Sufia — Carlos
   Wear Your Uniform
   You have to wear your uniform.
   Do I have to?
   Yes, it's a safety rule.

4. Sufia — Tony
   Can you work overtime next Saturday?
   On Saturday?
   Yes, I'd really appreciate it.
   All right.

5. Bao — Ted — José
   You can take your lunchbreak now.
   NATIONAL WIDGIT

6. Mike — Bao
   Can I leave early? I have a doctor's appointment.
   No problem. Go ahead.

D MAKE IT PERSONAL. Think about your English class. What does your English teacher ask or allow you to do? What do you persuade your teacher to do? On notepaper, write sentences with *make, have, let,* and *get.*

My teacher made us write a journal in English.

READ

Read the newspaper article. What two emergency situations are mentioned?

Workplace Safety Heroes Honored

Two local heroes, both employees of Rand Manufacturing, were honored with workplace safety awards.

Last April, Luis Rodriguez, a forty-four-year-old supervisor at Rand Manufacturing, gave CPR to fifty-two-year-old Sam Hue. On April 25, Hue was working on the assembly line when he **collapsed** and went unconscious. Realizing that Hue had suffered a heart attack, Rodriguez acted quickly, calling 911 and then starting heart **compressions** immediately. When paramedics arrived, they said that Rodriguez's actions had saved Hue's life.

Rodriguez only became a supervisor last March. He **credits** Rand's supervisor training, which includes first aid and CPR instruction, for allowing him to help Hue. He said, "Before March, I didn't know how to do CPR, so it was lucky I had that training." Hue, who was also at the awards ceremony, expressed his gratitude, saying, "I'm certainly thankful that Luis had that training, too. I wouldn't be here today if he hadn't."

The second hero, Jean Gross, is a thirty-eight-year-old security officer at Rand. On

June 20, Gross was working the night shift when a fire started in a chemical storage room. The fire alarm failed to work, but Gross noticed the fire while on his rounds and took quick action. First he manually **activated** the fire alarm, and then he closed the emergency doors to contain the fire before he finally left the building himself.

Fire Chief Bill Adams said that the fire would likely have been very serious without Gross's actions. Gross was **modest** when he accepted the award, saying, "I just did what I was taught in my training. They gave us steps to take in case of fire, and I remembered my training."

CHECK YOUR UNDERSTANDING

A Read the article again. Number the events from each award-winner's story in the order they happened.

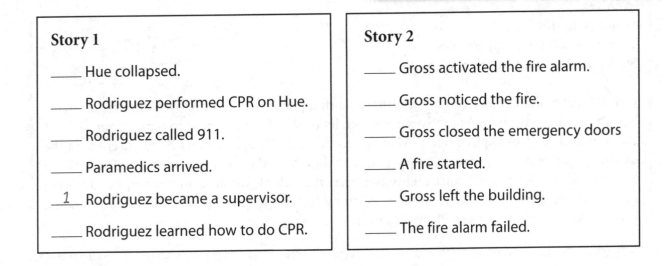

Story 1

_____ Hue collapsed.

_____ Rodriguez performed CPR on Hue.

_____ Rodriguez called 911.

_____ Paramedics arrived.

__1__ Rodriguez became a supervisor.

_____ Rodriguez learned how to do CPR.

Story 2

_____ Gross activated the fire alarm.

_____ Gross noticed the fire.

_____ Gross closed the emergency doors

_____ A fire started.

_____ Gross left the building.

_____ The fire alarm failed.

B Read the statements. Circle *True* or *False*.

1. Rodriguez and Gross work for the same company.	**True**	**False**
2. Rodriguez gave CPR to a customer.	**True**	**False**
3. Supervisors at Rodriguez's company are trained in CPR.	**True**	**False**
4. Gross is a firefighter.	**True**	**False**
5. The fire happened at night.	**True**	**False**
6. Gross was trained to handle fire emergencies.	**True**	**False**

C WORD WORK. Find the boldfaced words in the article. Match the words with the definitions.

1. _____ **collapse**

2. _____ **compression**

3. _____ **credit**

4. _____ **activate**

5. _____ **modest**

a. the act of pressing down hard

b. unwilling to talk proudly about your achievements

c. to make something start working

d. to give responsibility for something good

e. to fall down suddenly because of illness or injury

A Read the company memo. Circle the reflexive pronouns and underline the nouns they refer back to.

MEMO
From: Doug Torres
To: All assembly-line supervisors
Subject: Safety training for new employees

I would like to thank all of you for your hard work during our new employee orientation week. You should all be proud of yourselves. However, let us stop for a moment to remind ourselves of the importance of workplace safety. Many workers want to start working by themselves on the assembly line right away, but it's important that they have the right safety training first. We've had several new employees hurt themselves recently. I think we need to reassess our training procedures to ensure that we're doing everything we can to prevent injuries. I've revised the procedures myself, but I'd also like your input.

B Complete the sentences. Use the reflexive pronouns in the box.

> herself   himself   myself   ourselves
> themselves   yourself   yourselves

1. Ron tried to do all the work ___himself___, but he really needed help.

2. I wrote the employee safety guidelines _____.

3. We wear safety equipment to make sure we don't hurt _____.

4. If you start to fall, use the safety rail to catch _____.

5. Lily cut _____ on the new cutting machine, and she had to go to the hospital.

6. Everyone, please help _____ to cookies in the break room.

7. For the first week, new employees work with a trainer. After that, they work by _____.

C Complete the conversations. Circle the correct words.

1. **A:** Celia cut **(her)** / **herself** finger when she was opening boxes today. I think she hurt **her** / **herself** badly.

   B: Oh no! I hope she's OK.

2. **A:** My boss asked me to work by **my** / **myself** yesterday, but I told **him** / **himself** that I wasn't comfortable doing that.

   B: It's good that you told **him** / **himself**.

3. **A:** Can you move those boxes out of the hallway? Workers might trip over **them** / **themselves** and hurt **them** / **themselves**.

   B: You're right. I'll move them now.

4. **A:** Please don't use this machine by **you** / **yourself**. You need two people to operate it safely. You could injure **you** / **yourself**.

   B: OK, I understand.

5. **A:** Kai thought he could do this job by **him** / **himself**, but now he's not sure.

   B: I told **him** / **himself** it was too much work for one person!

D Read a nurse trainee's notes about her job. Correct four more mistakes.

> 4 P.M.—A young man with a bad burn came in. He burned ~~him~~ _{himself} on chemicals at his job in a factory. Dr. Silvan told himself that he needed to see a burn specialist.
>
> 5 P.M.—A father came in with his nine-year-old daughter who had a bad cut on her hand. The girl cut her when she was trying to help her father make dinner. The girl needed five stitches, and for the first time, Dr. Silvan let me put them in by my! She said I did a good job, so I was proud of me.

LIFE SKILLS

A Read the accident report. How many people must sign this report? _____

Palace Restaurant
Workplace Injury Report

Report accidents immediately and complete this form. Form must be submitted to your supervisor.

Name: _Mai Pham_   ☐ Male ☑ Female

Date of birth: _5/ 3/ 81_

Address: _3418 Smith Lane, Seattle, WA 98108_

Home phone: _206-555-4993_   Cell: _206-555-3007_

Employment start date: _8/13/ 2009_

Position: _lead chef_

Restaurant branch: _Palace Restaurant, 19th Ave. East, Seattle_

Location of accident: _same_

Date of accident: _2/25/2010_

Description of accident: _I was boiling water for rice. I was lifting a_
large pot, and it fell out of my hands. Hot water spilled on my right hand and down
my right leg.

Witness name and telephone number: _Jorge Martinez, 206-555-1186_

Description of injury: _burns on right hand and right leg_

_____

Was medical treatment sought?   ☐ Yes ☑ No

If yes, write doctor's name and address: _____

Number of days missed from work: _2_

Date of return to work: _2/28/2010_

Type of leave: _sick days_

Employee signature: _Mai Pham_   Date: _2/25/10_

Witness signature: _Jorge Martinez_   Date: _2/25/10_

Supervisor signature: _Lois Drake_   Date: _2/25/10_

B **Read the accident report again. Answer the questions.**

1. Where does Mai work? _____

2. When did the accident happen? _____

3. What was Mai doing when the accident happened? _____

4. Did Mai see a doctor for her injury? _____

5. How many days of work did Mai miss? _____

STUDY SKILL: Use a line graph

Look at the line graphs about workplace injuries. Answer the questions.

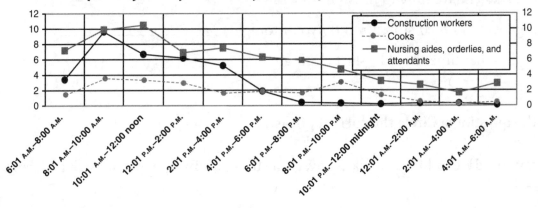

Workplace Injuries by Time of Day and Occupation (numbers in thousands)

Source: U.S. Bureau of Labor Statistics

1. What occupations are shown in the graph? _____

2. Which occupation had fewer than 1,000 injuries between 6:01 P.M. and 8:00 P.M.?

_____

3. At what time did nursing aides have the most workplace injuries? _____

4. At what time did construction workers have the least injuries? _____

5. How many injuries did cooks have from 12:01 P.M. to 2:00 P.M.? _____

A Complete the conversations. Unscramble the words to make a request, a suggestion, or an offer.

1. **A:** (I / you / could / to / this morning / talk) _____ Could I talk to you this morning? _____

   B: Yes, of course. Come to my office at ten o'clock.

2. **A:** (don't / now / why / take a break / you) _____

   B: OK, thanks. I'll just finish this first.

3. **A:** (mind / working / you / on Saturday / would) _____

   B: I'm sorry, but I can't. I'm working at my other job that day.

4. **A:** (don't / finish / this / for you / I / why) _____

   B: Thanks. I don't have time to finish it myself.

5. **A:** (closing / would / the / store / mind / you / tonight) _____

   B: Not at all. What time should I start closing?

B Complete the questions. Circle the correct phrases.

1. (Would you mind) / Could you working overtime tonight? Two people are sick and can't

   come in.

2. **Why don't / Could** I leave work five minutes early today? I've got a dentist's appointment.

3. **Could you / Would you mind** work an extra shift next weekend? We have to fill a big order.

4. **Why don't I / Could you** help you with your paperwork? It looks like you've got a lot.

5. I'm sorry, I can't trade shifts with you on Saturday. **Why don't you / Would you mind** ask

   Jim? He works on Saturday, too.

6. **Could Salvador / Would Salvador mind** take out the garbage before he clocks out?

7. **Would you mind / Could you** showing me where the break room is?

C Complete the conversations. Make requests, offers, or suggestions.

1. **A:** (**could / borrow**) _Could I borrow_ your employee handbook?

   B: Sorry, but I lost mine. (**why / look**) _____ online? I think it's on the company website.

2. **A:** (**could / help**) _____ me with this box? It's really heavy.

   B: Oh, I'm sorry. I hurt my back last week. (**why / ask**) _____ Marco?

   A: He's not here today.

   B: (**why / wait**) _____ until tomorrow? You don't need it today.

3. **A:** (**would mind / show**) _____ me how to use this machine?

   B: I'm sorry, I don't know how to use it, either. (**why / get**) _____ the manual?

   A: Good idea.

D Write a request, suggestion, or offer for each situation. Use *Could you, Could I / Why don't you / Why don't I,* or *Would you mind.* More than one answer may be possible.

1. You are working the afternoon shift this Sunday, but you want to attend a birthday party. You know that your coworker is not working on Sunday and wants extra hours.

   _Would you mind working my shift this Sunday?_____

2. Your coworker has too much work to finish today. You have some extra time.

   _____

3. You need some information in the employee manual. Your manager has the manual.

   _____

4. Your employees didn't clean up the work area when they finished work. You want them to be sure to clean up next time.

   _____

5. It is really slow at work today. Some of your workers could go home early.

   _____

A Read the e-mail. Write a *P* next to the paragraph that identifies a workplace safety problem. Write a *C* next to the paragraph that explains the cause of the problem. Write an *S* next to the paragraph that suggests a solution.

> **Writing Tip**
>
> When you write about a problem, follow these steps: 1. Identify the problem. 2. Explain the cause. 3. Suggest a solution.

From: Lance Gomez

To: Carrie Chu

Subject: Clutter around the assembly line

Dear Ms. Chu,

I've been a line supervisor for six months now, and I've noticed a safety issue near the assembly line. There is often a lot of clutter around the area, and I'm afraid we are going to have some injuries because of this. Last week, one of my employees tripped over some boxes and almost hurt herself badly.

The reason for the clutter is that we are using some new packing materials that take up more space. Workers pull out the material, but don't take the time to move extra material away from the line. Workers are so focused on getting the job done that they don't realize that this is a safety issue.

I think that all the line supervisors need to help workers understand this problem. I suggest we take a few minutes in the next meeting to explain this. Also, we could take five minutes every hour and have one person move all the clutter out of the area. I think this would be an easy and inexpensive way to prevent injuries near the assembly line.

B Read the paragraph. Correct four more mistakes.

I've been ^a^ student at this school for a few months now. I'm worried about a safety issue that I've noticed. There is only a few signs showing where exits are located, and those are difficult to see. I think this are dangerous. I knows this is because the building is very old. There were probably more signs, but now they're gone or difficult to see. I think the school should to put up more signs, especially on the staircase. This would be easy and inexpensive, and it would make the school a lot safer.

A Complete the chart. Use the words in the box. Add the correct prefix. Use a dictionary to check your answers.

> correct ~~employed~~ expensive
> healthy legal polite
> possible safe sanitary

Learning Strategy:
Note Prefixes and Suffixes

Pay attention to prefixes and suffixes. This will help you learn more about vocabulary.

1. un-	2. im-	3. in-	4. il-
unemployed			

B WORD WORK. Complete the sentences. Use the words from the chart in Exercise A.

1. Samuel was _unemployed_ for a while, but he found a job last week.

2. It is _____ for a company to pay less than the minimum wage.

3. Our boss thought it was _____ to finish the job today, but we managed to do it.

4. It is _____ to work in this area without safety equipment. You could be injured.

5. Many former warehouse workers are _____. They have problems with their backs because they didn't use safe lifting techniques.

6. Inspectors gave the restaurant a fine because the kitchen was _____. The kitchen staff was not cleaning the equipment properly.

7. A pair of safety glasses costs only about ten dollars. They are _____, but they could save your eyes from serious injury.

Unit 11: Know the Law!

A Read the sentences. Draw one line under the past continuous verbs that show action that was interrupted. Draw two lines under the simple past verbs that show the interrupting action.

1. I <u>was waiting</u> for my friend outside my apartment building when a police car <u>stopped</u> in front of the building. Three police officers went into the building where someone was having a party.

2. My father was taking the dog for a walk last night when he saw some teenagers. They were writing graffiti on a wall.

3. My son and his friend were riding the bus home from school when a fight started between two passengers. The fight was still going on when my son got off the bus.

B Complete the sentences. Circle the correct words.

1. While Faina **went** / **(was going)** through customs, the officer **asked** / **was asking** her to open her suitcase.

2. When my brother **walked** / **was walking** into the basement, some kids **tried** / **were trying** to break into the storage room.

3. Charlie **had** / **was having** a party when the neighbors **called** / **were calling** to complain about the noise.

4. I **noticed** / **was noticing** a young woman steal some perfume while I **shopped** / **was shopping** in the department store.

5. The teenagers **loitered** / **were loitering** in the hallway when the building manager **asked** / **was asking** them to leave.

C Complete the conversation. Use the simple past or the past continuous.

A: Tell me again what _____*happened*_____.
(**1. happen**)

B: Well, I _____ past the drugstore when
(**2. walk**)

suddenly I _____ someone shouting.
(**3. hear**)

And then I _____ this guy. . . .
(**4. see**)

A: What was he doing?

B: He _____ out of the store. And two of
(**5. run**)

the employees _____ him.
(**6. chase**)

A: Where did they go?

B: When I _____ them, they _____ towards the park.
(**7. see**)   (**8. run**)

D Unscramble the sentences. Use and the simple past and the past continuous
with *when* or *while.*

1. (I / cross the street / a police officer / stop me)

   when: _I was crossing the street when a police officer stopped me._____

2. (we / wait outside the store / get a ticket for loitering)

   while: _____

3. (Mrs. Jones / watch TV / hear about the accident)

   when: _____

4. (Ali / sit at a traffic light / a car / hit him from behind)

   while: _____

5. (someone / steal my purse / wait at the bus stop)

   when: _____

6. (two thieves / enter the store / Mr. Wong / work)

   while: _____

LIFE SKILLS

A Read the newspaper article. What crime was the defendant found guilty of? _____

Verdict Reached In Johnson Trial

In a stunning end to the trial of Dennis Johnson, a jury composed of seven men and five women found Johnson guilty of stealing approximately $50,000 over a period of five years while he was an employee of Greenville City and County. The jury deliberated for two days before agreeing on a verdict.

In the trial before Judge Vera Samuels, Johnson's defense attorney, Janine Smith, claimed that Johnson had been unaware that the money was missing. But Prosecutor Harry Garcia claimed that Johnson not only stole the money but also had worked out an elaborate plan to hide his tracks.

Several witnesses were called, including Johnson's ex-boss, Francine Wu, who had originally been named as a suspect in the case.

Johnson sat motionless and showed no emotion when the verdict was read.

B Read the article again. Then look at the picture. Label each person's role, using words in the box. Then write each person's name from the article.

> ~~defendant~~   defense attorney   judge
> prosecutor   witness

1. _defendant, Dennis Johnson_

2. _____

3. _____

4. _____

5. _____

DICTIONARY SKILL: Identify examples

A Read the dictionary entries. Notice the example sentences in italics and the boldface words. Then answer the questions.

> **ac•cuse** /əˈkyuz/ *v.* [T] to say that someone has done something wrong or illegal: *Norton was **accused of** murder.* | *Are you accusing me of cheating?*

> **crime** /kraɪm/ *n.* [U] illegal activities in general: | *There's very little crime in this neighborhood.* | *Women are less likely to **commit crime**.* | *methods of **crime prevention*** | *The **crime rate** has gone down in the last few years.* | ***Violent crime** is up by 8%.*

> **ev•i•dence** /ˈɛvədəns/ *n.* [U] facts, objects, or signs that show that something exists or is true: *the police **have evidence** that the killer was a woman.* | *scientists looking for **evidence of** life on other planets* | *I had to **give evidence** (= tell the facts) in my brother's trial.* | *The strongest **evidence for** the theory comes from ongoing studies of bacteria.* | *There was very little **evidence against** him.*

1. What is the first example sentence given in the *accuse* entry? _____

2. What preposition is commonly used **after** the word *accuse*? _____

3. What is the first example sentence given in the *crime* entry? _____

4. What verb is commonly used with the word *crime*? _____

5. What two nouns are commonly used **after** the word *crime*? _____

6. What adjective is commonly used **before** the word *crime*? _____

7. What is the first example sentence given in the *evidence* entry? _____

8. What three prepositions are commonly used **after** the word *evidence*? _____

9. What two verbs are commonly used with the word *evidence*? _____

B Complete the sentences. Circle the correct word.

1. There has been an increase in injury **crimes** / **violent crimes** in our area.

2. The **crime number** / **crime rate** is rising in many towns across the state.

3. If you are accused of **committing** / **making** a crime, you will need an attorney.

4. Several witnesses were called to **give** / **make** evidence at the trial.

5. The defendant was accused **for** / **of** the crime, but the case was dismissed because there was

   not enough evidence **against** / **for** him.

A Read the description of the jury selection process. Underline the examples of the passive voice.

When a citizen <u>is called</u> for jury duty, he or she must go to the court on a specific date. First, a prospective juror waits in a waiting room until his or her name is called. Then, the person is sent to the courtroom, where the prosecutor and the defense attorney are introduced, and where the prospective jurors are given some information about the trial. One by one, each individual is questioned to determine if he or she would be a suitable juror. If a juror has a good reason not to participate in the trial, he or she is excused and another name is called. This continues until all twelve juror seats are filled.

B Complete the news stories. Circle the correct words.

NEWS BRIEFS

STARSON APPEARS IN COURT

In a trial that **held** / (**was held**) today in Los Angeles, film star Lee Starson **accused** / **was accused** of shoplifting from a department store. Starson **appeared** / **was appeared** in court wearing sweatpants and a T-shirt. Several witnesses **called** / **were called**. However, the case **dismissed** / **was dismissed**.

LOCAL BUSINESSMAN ROBBED

Ron Delgado, owner of the Quik-bite restaurant chain, was the victim of a robbery last night at 11:15 P.M. Delgado **was returning** / **was returned** home from work when he **approached** / **was approached** by two men who **asked** / **was asked** him for money. When Mr. Delgado **refused** / **was refused**, he **knocked** / **was knocked** to the ground and his wallet **took** / **was taken**. The men **escaped** / **were escaped** in a gray van. Delgado **treated** / **was treated** for minor injuries at Greenville Hospital.

C Read the crime and court reports. Complete the sentences. Use the simple past passive.

Crime & Court Reports

6:36 A.M.   Police _____were called_____ to a home on Revere St.
             (1. call)
             Two men were involved in an argument. Both men

             _____ and charged with assault.
             (2. arrest)

7:15 A.M.   The principal of Lincoln Elementary school reported

             that the entry to the school yard _____
             (3. block)
             by city vehicles. The Department of Public Works

             _____ and the vehicles _____.
             (4. call)   (5. move)

7:50 A.M.   A motorcycle _____ missing on Wells
             (6. report)
             Avenue.

7:53 A.M.   Police received reports of two vehicles speeding on

             Highway 6. One car _____ and the driver,
             (7. stop)
             a resident of Halley Avenue, _____ with
             (8. charge)
             driving at an unsafe speed.

8:15 A.M.   The missing motorcycle _____ on Edgestone
             (9. find)
             Way and returned to the owner.

D Rewrite each sentence. Change the active voice to the passive voice.

1. Someone stole fifty dollars from my wallet. _Fifty dollars was stolen from my wallet._

2. The police arrested the suspects. _____

3. Someone damaged my car. _____

4. They scheduled a trial. _____

5. They called several witnesses. _____

6. A police officer brought in the defendant. _____

7. The people in the court heard the evidence. _____

8. The judge dismissed the case. _____

READ

Read the web page. Who was this page written for? _____

LAW OFFICES OF HWANG AND SAMUELS

Criminal Law:
Your Questions Answered
You may watch all the police and crime shows on TV, but do you know how the law really operates? Here are some of the questions that our clients have asked us recently. For more information about these or any other legal issues, contact our office at 1-800-555-6789.

Question: What happens if I am accused of a misdemeanor?
Answer: A misdemeanor is a less serious crime than a felony, so if you are found guilty of a misdemeanor, the most likely punishment is a fine, or maybe a short stay in prison. However, even though a misdemeanor is a less serious **offense**, a conviction can have a serious effect on your life. You should always take any charge against you seriously and seek the help of an experienced attorney.

Question: What is perjury?
Answer: A defendant can be found guilty of perjury if a jury can find that, in the course of a trial, he or she gave a knowingly false reply to a question; in other words, he or she lied on purpose when the truth could have been told. A perjury conviction can only take place if the false testimony is **relevant** to the case or might influence the jury.

Question: Who determines what punishment a convicted defendant receives?
Answer: It is the judge, not the jury, who **determines** the punishment, even after a jury trial. Only very occasionally do juries take part in the decision, notably in **capital punishment** cases. In some states, a judge cannot impose a death penalty without a jury recommendation.

Question: Do people convicted of the same crimes receive similar sentences?
Answer: Some crimes carry **mandatory** sentences, which require judges to impose similar or identical sentences on defendants who break these laws. However, many crimes do not carry mandatory sentences and allow the judge to take different factors into account, such as the defendant's past history, age, or circumstances.

CHECK YOUR UNDERSTANDING

A Look at the sentence. Break the sentence into seven "chunks." The first two have been done for you.

A defendant can be found guilty of perjury | if a jury can find that, | in the course of a trial, he or she gave a knowingly false reply to a question; in other words, he or she lied on purpose when the truth could have been told.

B Read the web page again. Complete the sentences.

1. If you are convicted of a _____, you will probably have to pay a fine or spend a short time in prison.

2. A _____ is a more serious type of crime than a misdemeanor.

3. If you are charged with any crime, it a good idea to get legal advice from an experienced _____.

4. If you knowingly tell a lie during testimony, you could be guilty of _____.

5. After a defendant have been found guilty, it is almost always the responsibility of a _____ to decide the punishment.

6. If a crime has a mandatory _____, the law requires that every defendant convicted of that crime receive the same punishment.

C WORD WORK. Find the boldface words in the article. Match the words with the definitions.

1. ____ **offense**   a. a sentence of death given for serious crimes

2. ____ **relevant**   b. to decide something

3. ____ **determine**   c. an illegal action or a crime

4. ____ **capital punishment**   d. must be done because of a rule or law

5. ____ **mandatory**   e. directly related to the subject being discussed

A **Read the first sentence. Then circle the statement that is closest in meaning.**

1. We can park here as long as we leave before 4 P.M.

   (a.) We can park the car here until 4 P.M.

   b. We can park here after 4 P.M.

2. You can't turn right on a red light, even if there aren't any cars coming.

   a. You can turn right if there are no cars.

   b. You can't turn right on a red light.

3. I got a ticket even though I wasn't speeding.

   a. I wasn't speeding; that's why I got a ticket.

   b. I wasn't speeding, but I got a ticket.

4. As long as you have insurance, you can rent a car.

   a. You can rent a car if you have insurance.

   b. You can rent a car even if you don't have insurance.

B **Complete the sentences. Circle the correct words.**

1. You can drive in the U.S. **as long as** / **even though** you have a valid driver's license.

2. Rick's parents won't let him use the car **as long as** / **even though** he has a license.

3. You can't cross the street when the walk light is red **even if** / **as long as** the street is empty.

4. **As long as** / **Even if** I drive carefully, I can borrow the car.

5. You can stop here **as long as** / **even though** you're not blocking traffic.

6. **Even if** / **Even though** the parking meter was broken, I still got a ticket.

7. You won't have to pay the ticket **as long as** / **even if** you get the headlight fixed.

8. You can't make a U-turn here **as long as** / **even if** there are no cars coming.

C Complete the sentences. Use *as long as*, *even if*, or *even though*.

In the U.S., most people start driving in their mid-teens, (1.) ___even though___ studies show that teens are much more likely than adults to be involved in accidents. In Washington State, for example, teenagers can get a driver's permit at the age of fifteen, (2.) _____ they are enrolled in a driver education program. Then they can get an intermediate driver's license, (3.) _____ they have completed fifty hours of supervised driving and have had a clean driving record for six months. They must have fifty hours of supervised driving experience (4.) _____ they have completed a driver education program. After all, (5.) _____ you pass a driver education course, you still need to practice driving in real conditions. (6.) _____ many teenagers are responsible and safe drivers, drivers between sixteen and nineteen years old are much more likely to have a car accident.

D Look at the pictures. Complete the sentences.

1. You don't have to stop at a crosswalk as long as _the crosswalk is empty._____

2. You can't turn left even if _____

3. You can park here as long as _____

4. That driver is double-parked even though _____

A Read the paragraph. Copy the chart below on notepaper. Complete the chart with information about the legal systems in the U.S. and Taiwan.

Writing Tip:
Compare and Contrast

When comparing and contrasting two things, use words such as similar, similarly, and like to signal similarities and words such as different and in contrast to signal differences.

There are some important differences between the legal systems in the U.S. and Taiwan. In Taiwan and in the U.S., people have the right to remain silent when they are being questioned by police. In both countries, people also have the right to have a lawyer with them during questioning.

In Taiwan there is a judge in each courtroom as there is in the U.S. However, in Taiwan, unlike in the U.S., there is no jury system; it is the judge who decides each case. Another difference is that in Taiwan, the judge questions the witnesses and the defendants, rather than defense attorneys or prosecutors. While attorneys are usually in the courtroom, they are not allowed to ask the witnesses questions.

The Legal Systems of the U.S. and Taiwan	
Taiwan	The U.S.
People can remain silent when questioned by police.	

B Read the paragraph. Find five more mistakes.

In Brazil, ^the first step in a legal process is a hearing, when the defendant goes before judge who listens to the prosecution and the defense. The aim of the hearing is to decide whether or not a case need to go to court. If the judge decide that a felony have been committed, and that there is enough evidence to prosecute defendant, he or she can set a date for a trial.

Review & Expand: Vocabulary

A Match the legal words with the definitions.

1. _e_ bail
2. ___ a felony
3. ___ loitering
4. ___ a misdemeanor
5. ___ a plea
6. ___ a sentence
7. ___ trespassing

a. a crime that is not very serious
b. a punishment that a judge gives
c. a statement made by a defendant saying whether he or she is guilty or not
d. entering someone's property without permission
e. money that a prisoner leaves to get out of jail before a trial
f. a serious crime, such as murder
g. the crime of staying in a place for a long time without a reason

Learning Strategy:
Write Definitions

Writing the definitions of new words will help you to remember the meanings. When you learn a new word, make a flashcard. Write the word on one side of the card and the definition on the other side.

B Complete the sentences. Use the words in the box.

arrested   committed   convicted   dismissed
found   pleaded   released   sued

1. The case was _dismissed_ because there wasn't enough evidence.

2. The police _____ my cousin for trespassing on someone's property. He was _____ after a couple of hours, but he had to pay a fine before they would let him go. He didn't even know that he had _____ a crime.

3. The defendant _____ not guilty, but the jury _____ him guilty. After the defendant was _____, the judge sentenced him to three years in prison.

4. My neighbor was injured when a tree fell on his car. He _____ the owner of the tree.

Ⓐ **Read the bank brochure. Then read the description of article usage and give two examples from the brochure.**

> **Online banking lets you manage your account.**
>
> > Setting up an online account is as easy as 1-2-3!
> > 1. Go to our website at www.123bank.net and complete the enrollment form.
> > 2. Choose a user name and a password.
> > 3. Once you have the password, you will be able to access your account.
>
> If you need assistance, call 1-800-555-4567 to speak to a representative.

1. An indefinite article (*a/an*): _an online account, a user name_

2. A definite article (*the*): _____

3. No article: _____

4. A possessive article: _____

Ⓑ **Complete the conversation. Circle the correct answers. (Ø means no article is necessary.)**

A: I'd like some information about applying for ⓐ/ **the** credit card.

B: Of course. Here's **a** / **Ø** brochure that describes **a** / **the** cards that we offer.

A: What is **Ø** / **the** interest rate on the rewards card? I want to get **a** / **Ø** cash back.

B: Well, I can offer you **an** / **Ø** introductory rate of 1 percent. After three months, **an** / **the** interest rate will be between 10 and 20 percent, depending on your credit rating. I think you'll find that our **the** / **Ø** rates are very competitive.

A: OK, thanks. I'll take a look at **a** / **the** brochure and get back to you.

C Complete the paragraph about credit cards. Use *a*, *an*, *the*, or Ø.

Even if you usually pay with __Ø__ cash or use ____ checks to buy things, it's ____ good idea to build ____ strong credit history. If you have good credit, it is easier to get ____ loan for things like ____ car, ____ computer, or even ____ new home. Also, ____ employers may check your credit because ____ good credit history shows that you are ____ responsible person. ____ Most landlords also check your credit because it tells them whether you will pay your ____ rent on time. Credit cards let you buy items online and over ____ phone, and you do not have to carry a lot of ____ cash. And finally, credit cards are good to have in ____ emergencies.

D Read the conversation. Correct eight more errors by adding articles, crossing out articles, or changing articles.

Customer:	I'm starting my own business. I'd like information about ~~a~~ business loans.
Loan Officer:	Sure. Can you tell me a little about business you're starting?
Customer:	Well, it's small grocery store.
Loan Officer:	So you'll probably need to buy equipment like the cash register and the freezer. We offer equipment loan that would be a good choice for you. You can pay back loan in fixed monthly payments.
Customer:	That sounds good. How do I apply for that?
Loan Officer:	Here's a brochure about a loans that we offer, and here is an application form. I'll help you fill out a form if you like.

E MAKE IT PERSONAL. Are credit cards a good idea? Explain your answer.

_____

_____

READ

Read the article. What is the purpose of the article?

Choosing a Credit Card

There are many credit cards out there, with many different features. Of course, every credit card company will try to make its card seem attractive to you! So, how do you choose **wisely**? Here are some important questions to ask:

How are you going to use your credit card?

The first step in choosing a card is deciding how you will use it. If you plan to pay your balance in full every month, your best choice may be a card that has no annual fee and offers a longer grace period for payment. If you know that you will **carry over** your balance from month to month, a card with a lower interest rate (stated as an annual percentage rate, or APR) may be a good choice. If you want to use the card for cash advances, look for a lower APR and lower fees on cash advances. Note that many cards charge a higher rate for cash advances than for **purchases**.

What are the APRs?

A single card may have several APRs: one for purchases, one for cash advances, and one for balance transfers. APRs can change, so check this information carefully. Companies often offer an introductory APR at a very low rate. This low rate goes up after a certain period of time—sometimes to a much higher rate.

What are the fees?

It's important to find out what fees can be charged. Some typical fees include an annual fee, a cash advance fee, a balance-transfer fee, and a late payment fee. Try to avoid cards with high fees.

How long is the grace period?

The grace period is the number of days you have to pay your bill in full. Most cards have grace periods of twenty or twenty-five days. Not paying the full amount of your bill will result in a finance charge. The grace period usually applies only to new **purchases**. Most credit cards do not give a grace period for cash advances and balance transfers.

Does the card offer incentives?

Many credit card companies offer **incentives** to use the card and other special features. These might include **rebates** on purchases, frequent flier miles, or car rental insurance. Remember that you will usually pay for these features in some way. For example, a card that offers rebates may have an annual fee.

CHECK YOUR UNDERSTANDING

A Check (✓) the best summary of the article.

❏ Choosing a credit card is a difficult process, and companies will send you alot of information to get you to choose their card.

❏ There are a lot of choices with credit cards. It's important to get information before you make your choice.

Reading Skill:
Summarizing

Write a summary to show that you understand what you've read. Include the main idea and the most important information in the text.

B Read the article again. Answer the questions.

1. What kind of card is best if you always pay your balance in full? _____

2. What kind of card is best if you carry a balance? _____

3. What is an APR? _____

4. What are four fees that a credit card company can charge? _____

5. What is a grace period? _____

6. What are three incentives that a credit card can offer? _____

C WORD WORK. Find the boldface words in the article. Complete the sentences with the boldface words.

1. I never _____ the balance on my credit card. I always pay the full balance.

2. Harry spends his money _____. He thinks carefully every time he opens his wallet.

3. My wife prefers to pay for _____ with her credit card. She hates to carry cash.

4. Many stores offer frequent shopper cards. These cards encourage shoppers to spend more money with _____ such as discounts and free gifts.

5. My credit card gives me 1 percent cash back every time I buy something. In a year, those _____ add up to a lot of money!

Lessons 4 & 5: Grammar

A Complete the sentences. Match the *if* clauses with the correct result clauses.

1. _e_ If you keep track of expenses,

2. ___ If you don't go out as often,

3. ___ If you walk to school,

4. ___ If you eat at home,

5. ___ If you don't talk on the phone so much,

6. ___ If you save a little each month,

a. your bill will be lower.

b. it will add up over time.

c. you'll save money on entertainment.

d. you won't spend money on the bus.

e. you'll know how much you're spending.

f. you'll save money on food.

B Read the magazine article. Complete the sentences. Circle the correct words.

A Penny Saved Is a Penny Earned

Do you think it's hard to save money? It's easier than you think! Follow our tips and you'll be surprised at how much you can save.

Make a budget. Many people don't realize how important this is! If you **don't** / **won't** know how much money you need, you **don't** / **won't** be able to plan for saving.

Watch the little things. It's easy to spend a lot of money on a lot of little things: coffee, snacks, etc. **You / You'll** be surprised at how much you can save if you **don't** / **won't** spend so much on little things.

Add it up. Our grandparents knew this but many of us have forgotten. If **you / you'll** save even a few pennies, **they / they'll** add up over time. Really, it's true!

C Complete the conversation. Use the future real conditional.

Nina: This is terrible. We aren't saving any money. If we ___*don't cut*___ down on

___(1. not / cut)___

our spending, we _____ enough to buy a house.

___(2. not / save)___

Leonid: Well, if we _____ the car, we _____ some money to

___(3. sell)___   ___(4. have)___

put in our savings account.

Nina: Right. But, if we _____ rid of the car, you _____ to

___(5. get)___   ___(6. have)___

spend a lot more time commuting. You _____ less time with the

___(7. spend)___

family if you _____ to spend all that time on the train.

___(8. have)___

Leonid: True. What about cable TV? If we _____ our subscription,

___(9. cancel)___

we _____ almost $60.

___(10. save)___

Leonid: Good idea. That's not enough for a house, but it's a good start!

D Antonio wants to pay off his debts. Look at the chart. On notepaper, write
five sentences about his ideas and possible results. Use the future real
conditional.

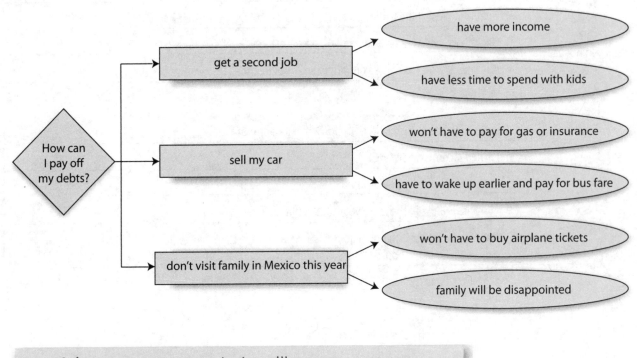

If Antonio gets a second job, he'll have more income.

LIFE SKILLS

A Read the W-2 form. How much money did the employee earn this year? _____

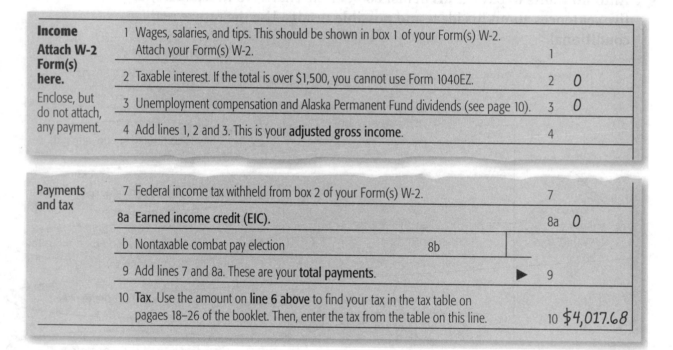

a Employee's social security number		Safe, accurate, FAST! Use	**IRS e file**	Visit the IRS website at www.irs.gov/efile.
333-00-5544	OMB No. 1545-0008			

b Employer identification number (EIN) 33-0005555	1 Wages, tips, other compensation $32,084	2 Federal income tax withheld $6,372.54
c Employer's name, address, and ZIP code Clean Well 3489 West 7th Street Pittsburgh, PA 15122	3 Social security wages $32,084	4 Social security tax withheld $1,176.34
	5 Medicare wages and tips $32,084	6 Medicare tax withheld $749.55

B Look at the sections of the 1040EZ form. Use the information on the W-2 form in Exercise A to complete lines 1, 4, 7, and 9.

Income **Attach W-2 Form(s) here.** Enclose, but do not attach, any payment.	1 Wages, salaries, and tips. This should be shown in box 1 of your Form(s) W-2. Attach your Form(s) W-2.	1	
	2 Taxable interest. If the total is over $1,500, you cannot use Form 1040EZ.	2	0
	3 Unemployment compensation and Alaska Permanent Fund dividends (see page 10).	3	0
	4 Add lines 1, 2 and 3. This is your **adjusted gross income**.	4	

Payments and tax	7 Federal income tax withheld from box 2 of your Form(s) W-2.	7	
	8a **Earned income credit (EIC).**	8a	0
	b Nontaxable combat pay election 8b		
	9 Add lines 7 and 8a. These are your **total payments**. ▶	9	
	10 **Tax.** Use the amount on **line 6 above** to find your tax in the tax table on pagaes 18–26 of the booklet. Then, enter the tax from the table on this line.	10	$4,017.68

C Look at the W-2 and 1040EZ forms again. Answer the questions.

1. What is the name of the company that the employee works for? _____

2. What is the employer's identification number? _____

3. How much federal tax did the employee pay? _____

4. Which box on the W-2 form lists the Social Security withholding? _____

5. How much is the employee's adjusted gross income? _____

6. Which line on the 1040EZ lists the employee's total payments? _____

STUDY SKILL: Use a pie chart

Look at the pie charts. Answer the questions.

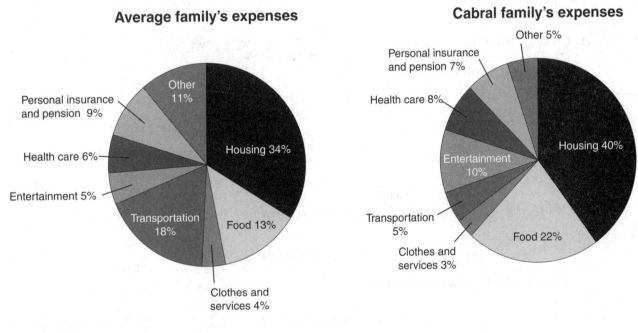

Average family's expenses

Other 11%
Personal insurance and pension 9%
Health care 6%
Entertainment 5%
Transportation 18%
Housing 34%
Food 13%
Clothes and services 4%

Cabral family's expenses

Other 5%
Personal insurance and pension 7%
Health care 8%
Entertainment 10%
Transportation 5%
Housing 40%
Food 22%
Clothes and services 3%

Source: U.S. Bureau of Labor Statistics

1. What are the two biggest expenses for the average family? _____

2. What is the smallest expense for the average family? _____

3. What are the two biggest expenses for the Cabral family? _____

4. What is the smallest expense for the Cabral family? _____

5. What four expenses does the Cabral family spend more than average on? _____

A Complete the sentences. Match the *if* clauses with the correct result clauses.

1. __e__ If I won the lottery,

2. ____ If I went back to school,

3. ____ If I got a raise at work,

4. ____ If I traveled a lot,

5. ____ If I didn't have to work,

a. I'd have time to travel a lot.

b. I'd pay off my debts.

c. I could learn a new career.

d. I'd see a lot of interesting places and meet interesting people.

e. I'd quit my job.

B Complete the conversations. Use the present unreal conditional. Use *would* in the results clause.

1. **A:** I wish I could quit my job. If I ___didn't have to___ work, I _____
   (not / have to)   **(have)**
   more time to do other things.

   B: Yes, but if you _____ your job, you _____ any money.
                           (quit)   **(not / make)**
   And, you _____ bored if you _____ .
              (be)   **(not / work)**

2. **A:** If Victor and I _____ more money, we _____ the
                          (have)   **(take)**
   children to see my parents in Poland next summer. But, we can't afford it.

   B: If you _____ saving now, maybe you _____ enough
                 (start)   **(have)**
   money saved by next summer.

3. **A:** If I _____ more money, I _____ back to school and get
              (have)   **(go)**
   my degree. If I _____ a college degree, I _____ for a
                    (have)   **(look)**
   higher-paying job.

   B: Maybe you will win the lottery. If you _____ rich, you
                                                (be)
   _____ able to go to any school you wanted to!
   (be)

C **Look at the pictures. Write sentences about the things the people would do. Use the present unreal conditional.**

1. In-Su
2. Tatiana
3. Gail and Paul
4. Safiya

1. (some extra money) <u>If In-Su had some extra money, he'd visit his family in Korea.</u>

2. (more experience) _____

3. (work fewer hours) _____

4. (speak better English) _____

D **MAKE IT PERSONAL. What would you do in these situations? Complete the sentences with your own dreams.**

1. If I didn't have to work, _____.

2. If I were rich, _____.

3. If I had more free time, _____.

A Read the paragraph. Circle the question that focuses the paragraph. Circle the answer to the question. Then underline three supporting details.

> **Writing Tip:** Asking and Answering a Question
>
> One way to focus a paragraph is to ask a question and answer it. You not only give an answer, you also explain your answer by giving supporting details such as facts and examples.

Which organization would I choose if someone gave me $1,000 and told me to give it to charity? I would give the money to Heifer International. This international organization was started in 1944 and works to end hunger and poverty and also to protect the earth. Its approach is interesting because it doesn't give poor families food or money. Instead, it gives them animals, such as cows, pigs, or chickens, that will make food for a long time. They also give the families training in how to care for the animals. This means that Heifer International helps poor families in a more long-term way than many other organizations. Poverty is one of the most serious problems in our world today, so this is why I would give the money to Heifer International.

B Read the paragraph. Correct five more mistakes.

If someone gave me $1,000 and told me to give the money away, ~~who I would~~ *who would I* give it to? I give the money to my local homeless shelter. I think it are important to focus charity on local problems because that is where individuals can make the most difference. My community have a big problem with homelessness, and there are several shelters that do good work. But the shelters never has enough money, so I would gave my money to one of these shelters.

Review & Expand: Vocabulary

A Read the definitions. Then read the sentences. Put an (✗) by the sentence that contains a mistake.

> borrow = you borrow something <u>from</u> someone
>
> lend = you lend something <u>to</u> someone

❑ 1. My friend Tia lent me her cell phone so I could call home.

❑ 2. I lent my computer from my friend Tia to do my homework.

❑ 3. I borrowed twenty dollars from my friend Tia, and I'm going to pay her back tomorrow.

B Complete the sentences. Use the words in the box.

> | | | | |
> |---|---|---|---|
> | account balance | ~~budget~~ | cut down on | debit card |
> | interest rate | minimum balance | online banking | overdraft |

1. It's a good idea to have a _____budget_____ so you can plan how much money you need.

2. You have an _____ when you write a check for more than you have in your account.

3. Check the _____ before you get a credit card. Some can be very high.

4. If you want to save money, you need to _____ your expenses.

5. _____ is convenient; you don't have to go to the bank.

6. Keep track of your _____ so you know how much money you have.

7. When you buy something with a _____, the money is taken directly from your bank account.

8. With some bank accounts, you have to maintain a _____. If the money in your account falls below that amount, you may be charged a fee.

Answer Key

TO THE STUDENT

Page v, Exercise A

Lessons 1 & 2: grammar
Lesson 3: reading
Lessons 4 & 5: grammar
Lesson 6: life skills and study skills
Lessons 7 & 8: grammar
Lesson 9: writing
Review & Expand: vocabulary

Page v, Exercise B

1. 4   2. 9   3. 12   4. 13

Page v, Exercise C

Dictionary Skill: Understand words with more than one meaning

Page v, Exercise D

1. answers to workbook exercises
2. *Answers will vary* means that students will write different answers. There is not a single, correct answer.

UNIT 1

Page 2, Exercise A

Alex: Excuse me. **Does the 52 stop** / **Is the 52 stopping** here?

Rosa: Yes, I wait / **I'm waiting** for the 52. Hey . . . Alex! **Do you remember** / **Are you remembering** me?

Alex: Rosa! Long time no see! How are you?

Rosa: I'm fine. But what **do you do** / **are you doing** here?

Alex: I work right across the street: over at Tito's.

Rosa: Really? That's funny. **I take** / I'm taking this bus every day, but **I never see** / I'm never seeing you.

Alex: Oh, **I don't usually take** / I'm not usually taking the bus. I usually drive to work. **I ride** / **I'm riding** the bus today because my wife **uses** / **is using** the car.

Rosa: Oh, I see.

Alex: What about you? What **do you do** / **are you doing** these days?

Rosa: Well, I take / **I'm taking** classes at the community center. **I want** / **I'm wanting** to get my GED.

Page 3, Exercise B

1. **A:** are you doing
   B: 'm going / 'm studying
   A: Do you like
2. **A:** are you doing
   B: 'm waiting / 's giving
3. **A:** do you do
   B: don't have / 'm working
4. **A:** 'm taking
   B: are you studying
   A: want

Page 3, Exercise C

1. do   3. Do   5. do   7. Are
2. Do   4. Are   6. do   8. Are

Page 4, BEFORE YOU READ

In the article, people talk about their belief in the American dream.

Page 4, READ

Circle: Barbara Monteza, Brian Miller

Page 5, Exercise A

1. True   3. False   5. False
2. True   4. True   6. True

Page 5, Exercise B

Answers will vary.

Page 5, Exercise C

1. c   2. b   3. a   4. a

Page 6, Exercise A

1. She's meeting *or* going to meet with an advisor.
2. She's working *or* going to work.
3. She's taking *or* going to take an accounting class.
4. She's meeting *or* going to meet Carlos at the library.
5. She's starting *or* going to start work at one o'clock.
6. She's studying *or* going to study for a test.
7. She's working *or* going to work from 11:00 to 7:00.
8. She's attending *or* going to attend a job fair.

Page 7, Exercise B

1. **B:** are getting
   A: are you going to have
   B: are having / are going to come
   A: 'll be
2. **A:** is having
   A: 're going to go
   B: 'll bring

Page 7, Exercise C

1. I'm going to go
2. I'm going to do
3. I'll study
4. I'm going to show
5. I'll get
6. are you going to stay
7. I'll go
8. I'll wait

Page 8, Exercise A

two

Page 9, Exercise B

1. Newby College
2. Esther Poon
3. Management in the Hotel Industry, Accounting Principles
4. her social security number, birthdate, name, gender, address, email address, phone numbers, and citizenship
5. a check or money order
6. submit to the Registrar's Office, fax to 651-555-8003, or enroll online

Page 9, Exercise C

Answers will vary.

Page 9, STUDY SKILL

1. $740   2. $428   3. $383

Page 10, Exercise A

1. was
2. came
3. lived
4. didn't speak
5. took
6. worked
7. turned
8. moved
9. got
10. didn't like
11. was
12. wasn't
13. decided
14. fell
15. were
16. said
17. didn't think
18. studied

Page 10, Exercise B

1. When did you come to the U.S.?
2. Where did you go to school?
3. How long did you work at Telemax?
4. What kind of work did you do?
5. Did you like that job?

Page 11, Exercise C

1. was
2. was
3. lived
4. was
5. did you live
6. owned
7. was
8. were
9. Did you work
10. didn't go
11. stayed
12. took
13. did you do
14. cleaned
15. bought
16. made
17. Did you have
18. went

Page 11, Exercise D

Answers will vary, but could include:

1. Selma used to live in a city with warm weather, but now she lives in a cold city.
2. She used to live in a house, but now she lives in an apartment.
3. She didn't use to go out to work, but now she works in a hotel.
4. She didn't use to drive, but now she has a car.
5. She used to cook a meal every day, but now she doesn't have time to cook.

Page 12, Exercise A

1. He came to the U.S. from Haiti in 1998.
2. He started taking English classes in 1999.
3. Sometimes he studied until two in the morning.
4. In 2005, he started working in a local hospital.

Page 12, Exercise B

My role model is my husband's grandmother. Grandma Li ~~come~~ **came** to the US from China and ~~raise~~ **raised** five children here. She didn't speak English, but she valued education and ~~make~~ **made** sure all the children worked hard in school. No one in the family had gone to college before, but all five of her children are college graduates. Now, her children are grown and Grandma Li finally ~~have~~ **has** time to study English. She ~~take~~ **takes** classes and also volunteers at the elementary school.

Page 13, Exercise A

Answers will vary, but could include:

Ali wanted a new job, so he started to do research. He attended a job search workshop. At the workshop, he learned about a job opening at a hotel. He sent in an application. A few weeks later, he had an interview. They called him the next day and he got the job!

Page 13, Exercise B

1. determined
2. successful
3. ambitious
4. hardworking
5. dependable
6. disciplined
7. goal-oriented

UNIT 2

Page 14, Exercise A

	infinitive to go	gerund going
I wanted	✓	
They like	✓	✓
We decided	✓	
Let's discuss		✓
She started	✓	✓
He recommended		✓
I need	✓	
You would like	✓	✓
She enjoys		✓
We prefer	✓	✓
They continued	✓	✓
He hopes	✓	

Page 14, Exercise B

Soo-Jin: How was your meeting at the job center today?

Luis: Good. We discussed **to set** / (**setting**) short-term and long-term goals. I'm going to finish **to work** / (**working**) on them tonight. But, I'm getting a little worried.

Soo-Jin: Why?

Luis: I'd like (**to wait**) / **waiting** for the right job, but I need (**to make**)/ **making** money soon.

Soo-Jin: Maybe you should consider **to find** /(**finding**) a part-time job and then you can continue (**to look**)/(**looking**) in your free time.

Luis: Maybe you're right. I'd really like (**to find**)/ **finding** something in my field, though.

Soo-Jin: Maybe you can find something in your field. You won't know until you start (**to look**)/(**looking**).

Page 15, Exercise C

Hi Luis,

I don't know if you've begun **to** look for a job yet, but I heard about a part-time customer service rep position at Allied Electric. A friend of mine works there and told me about the position. I thought of you because you enjoy ~~to work~~ **working** with people! I know you want ~~finding~~ **to find** a full-time position, but this might be a start. You could start ~~work~~ **working** part time, get some experience, and apply for more hours later. She thinks it's a good company and enjoys ~~to work~~ **working** there. I think you should consider ~~to send~~ **sending** in your résumé.

Gail

Page 15, Exercise D

Answers will vary.

Page 16, Exercise A

1. Objective
2. Qualifications
3. Related Experience
4. Achievements
5. Education

Page 17, Exercise B

1. False
2. False
3. True
4. True
5. False
6. True

Page 17, STUDY SKILL

1. calling employers by telephone
2. placing or answering ads on the Internet
3. Mailing a resume to employers
4. 24 percent
5. 33 percent

Page 18, Exercise A

1. I'm interested in applying for the sales job.
2. Linh is capable of managing other employees.
3. We're looking forward to hiring some new employees.
4. Is Gebru planning on finishing his degree soon?
5. Alicia is excited about starting her new position.

Page 18, Exercise B

1. starting
2. doing
3. not making
4. practicing
5. applying
6. working
7. owning
8. cooking

Page 19, Exercise C

1. working
2. quitting
3. staying
4. doing
5. using
6. fixing
7. having

Page 19, Exercise D

Answers will vary, but could include:

1. Jin-Sil is interested in working with people.
2. She is capable of supervising other workers.
3. She is good at solving problems.
4. She is planning on going back to school in the future.

Page 20, READ

Circle: quid pro quo sexual harassment, behavior of a sexual nature that leads to a hostile work environment

Page 20, Exercise A

d

Page 21, Exercise B

1. unwanted physical contact
2. sexual comments or jokes
3. displays of offensive materials such as pornography
4. repeated invitations for dates after being rejected

Page 21, Exercise C

1. True
2. False
3. True
4. True
5. False
6. True
7. True

Page 21, Exercise D

1. e
2. c
3. d
4. b
5. a

Page 22, Exercise A

1. have you worked
2. have worked
3. have had
4. have you done
5. have worked
6. have supervised
7. Have you ever done
8. haven't worked

Page 22, Exercise B

1. **A:** have never worked
   B: have
2. **A:** has worked
   B: started
3. **A:** did you get
   B: started
4. **A:** have you known
   B: met / have been
5. **A:** got
   B: has worked

Page 23, Exercise C

1. have lived
2. started
3. was
4. worked
5. got
6. studied
7. worked
8. wanted
9. have been
10. decided
11. have taken
12. have gotten
13. haven't worked
14. have worked

Page 23, Exercise D

Answers will vary, but could include:

1. Victor has been in the U.S. since September 2001.
2. He got a job at a shoe factory in October 2001.
3. He left the job at the shoe factory in August 2005.
4. He has worked at a hospital since September 2005.

Page 24, Exercise A

The following sentences should be crossed out:

1. My supervisor's name was Jim Matz, and I really enjoyed working for him.
2. I love the outdoors and enjoy hiking, camping, and canoeing.
3. A part-time position would be perfect for me while I work on my law degree.

Page 24, Exercise B

I **am** sending you my résumé in response to your ad for a part-time administrative assistant in today's *Daily Tribune*. I would like **to** apply for the position because I have a lot of administrative experience and I am interested **in** learning about the law profession.

I have ~~work~~ **worked** in three different offices. I ~~receive~~ **received** my bachelor's degree last year and am considering applying to law school.

Page 25, Exercise A

Answers will vary, but could include:

of: afraid, capable, tired
about: concerned, worried, excited
at: good, skilled, angry
in: believe, interested, majored

Page 25, Exercise B

Verb	Noun	Noun (person)
develop	development	developer
know	knowledge	X
require	requirement	X
respond	response	X
assist	assistance	assistant
apply	application	applicant

1. requirement
2. develop
3. assistance
4. knowledge
5. response
6. apply

UNIT 3

Page 26, Exercise A

1. about
2. with *or* about
3. of
4. in
5. with
6. about
7. at *or* with

Page 26, Exercise B

Hong: How do you like your new neighborhood?

Karine: Well, we've only been here a few weeks, but it's interested / (interesting). I'm (amazed) / amazing by all the shops and restaurants.

Hong: That sounds good. Are your neighbors friendly?

Karine: Well, I'm not sure. I am a little (frustrated) / frustrating because no one says hello. But there is a block party next week, so that will be interested / (interesting).

Hong: A block party? That sounds fun.

Karine: Yeah. My son is very (excited) / exciting. He really wants to meet some other kids.

Hong: Are there any other children in your building?

Karine: No. My son was very (disappointed) / disappointing about that.

Page 27, Exercise C

1. exciting
2. embarrassed
3. disappointed
4. frightened
5. confused
6. interested

Page 27, Exercise D

When my grandparents moved into a new apartment building, they were a little worried ~~for~~ **about** the neighbors. There were a lot of teenagers who were loud and a little ~~frightened~~ **frightening**. One night, my grandparents got back home and realized they didn't have their apartment keys. They were too ~~embarrassing~~ **embarrassed** to knock on a neighbor's door and ask for help. Suddenly, a teenage boy came into the building. He was big and scary looking. My grandmother was terrified. Then, the boy smiled and offered to help them. He called the building manager on his cell phone and waited until they got into their apartment. My grandparents were surprised ~~for~~ **at** his kindness, and very relieved! Since then, the boy stops over regularly to see if he can help my grandparents. He isn't so ~~terrified~~ **terrifying** after all.

Page 28, Exercise A

Sequoia Park

Page 28, Exercise B

Answers will vary, but could include:

1. Take Route 120 east to Locust Avenue.
2. Take the exit for Locust Avenue.
3. Drive north on Locust Avenue to Wawona Street.
4. Turn left on Wawona Street.
5. Sequoia Park is on your left.

Page 28, Exercise C

Answers will vary.

Page 29, Exercise A

1. IN A STORE ETC: The food is terrific, but the service is lousy. *or* the customer service department
2. WORK DONE: He retired after 20 years of service. *or* You may need the services of a lawyer. *or* She was given an award in honor of her years of service to the Democratic Party.
3. BUSINESS: a cleaning service
4. PUBLIC SERVICES: The new budget will cut city services such as trash collection and library hours.

Page 29, Exercise B

1. Meaning: 2
2. Meaning: 3
3. Meaning: 4
4. Meaning: 3
5. Meaning: 1
6. Meaning: 4
7. Meaning: 1

Page 30, Exercise A

1. wouldn't play
2. would turn
3. were *or* would be
4. would answer
5. didn't have
6. had

Page 30, Exercise B

Answers will vary, but could include:

1. I had a larger apartment
2. there was a playground in the neighborhood
3. he had a friend in the building
4. he lived closer to his work
5. they lived in our area
6. she had a job
7. the neighborhood were safer
8. his building had a parking lot

Page 31, Exercise C

Answers will vary, but could include:

Sam wishes he had a place to play soccer.
Barbara wishes she had a garage.
Francisco wishes he had a large garden.
Jenny wishes she were on a cruise.
Mei-Feng wishes the bus would come.

Page 31, Exercise D

Answers will vary.

Page 32, READ

c

Page 33, Exercise A

1. He owned a gardening business.
2. He wanted to help young people go to college.
3. Clients of his gardening business donated money.
4. The foundation gives scholarships and information about college to students.
5. The foundation gave Gloria a scholarship so that she could travel to classes at a college further away.

Page 33, Exercise B

1. True
2. False
3. True
4. False
5. True
6. False

Page 33, Exercise C

1. c   2. d   3. e   4. a   5. b

Page 34, Exercise A

Dear friend,
I <u>am asking you to vote</u> for me. Why? You <u>expect your politicians to know</u> your neighborhood. I have lived and worked in this city for twenty years. You <u>want the city to improve</u> services. As your representative, I will <u>urge the city to expand</u> after-school programs for our children. I will <u>ask the city council to increase</u> funding for street cleaning and recycling programs. <u>Remind your neighbors to vote</u> on November 4. <u>Tell them to vote</u> for me!

Page 34, Exercise B

1. The politician asked us to vote for him.
2. The instructor taught him to resist an attack.
3. We didn't expect her to call a meeting.
4. How would you like them to help you?
5. The police officers encouraged us to start a community group.
6. We're advising you to lock your doors.

Page 35, Exercise C

1. Officer Saland urged us to keep our eyes open.
2. She would like us to call the police if we see anything suspicious.
3. She advised us not to carry a lot of cash.
4. She encouraged us to walk home with a friend if possible.
5. She told us to walk in well-lit areas.
6. She reminded us to stay aware of our surroundings, especially at night.

Page 35, Exercise D

Answers will vary, but could include:

1. teens to find jobs
2. seniors to defend themselves
3. residents to get to know each other
4. children to look both ways before crossing the street

Page 36, Exercise A

1. People walk to and from the subway, even quite late at night.
2. My bank is around the corner, and there is even a post office just a few blocks away.
3. My neighbors always say hello and ask me how I'm doing when I walk by.

Page 36, Exercise B

When my wife and I first came to this neighborhood, we were ~~disappointing~~ **disappointed**. There was a lot of garbage on the street and graffiti. We wished that the street ~~looks~~ **looked** nicer. But then we formed a neighborhood group and we asked people ~~joining~~ **to join** us. At first people weren't ~~interesting~~ **interested,** but little by little they volunteered to help. We cleaned the graffiti and planted trees on the sidewalk. Now the streets look much better, and we are very ~~exciting~~ **excited** about what we have achieved. I would encourage everybody ~~doing~~ **to do** what we did. It really works!

Page 37, Exercise A

Answers will vary, but could include:

Neighborhood problems	Things at a street fair
graffiti	music
potholes	crafts
trash	entertainment
crime	food
no parking	games
noise	traditional dancing
no bus service	contests

Page 37, Exercise B

1. council
2. field
3. citizens
4. programs
5. center
6. collection

Page 37, Exercise C

1. city council
2. baseball field
3. community center
4. after-school programs
5. senior citizens
6. trash collection

UNIT 4

Page 38, Exercise A

1. figure out
2. get over
3. point out
4. count on
5. put together
6. help out
7. show up
8. hand out

Page 39, Exercise B

1. together
2. over
3. out
4. off
5. up
6. out
7. over
8. on

Page 39, Exercise C

1. Javier and I talked them over.
2. We figured it out.
3. Could you please help her out?
4. I put them together for the new project.
5. Let's bring it up at the staff meeting.
6. He signed him up for extra shifts.
7. We looked it up in the policy manual.

Page 40, Exercise A

☑ working overtime
☑ changing your dental plan
☐ holiday time off
☐ dates for being paid
☑ paid time off
☑ vacation request forms

Page 41, Exercise B

1. True
2. False
3. True
4. True
5. False

Page 41, STUDY SKILL

1. life insurance
2. childcare assistance
3. 60 percent
4. 49 percent
5. medical care
6. vacation pay

Page 42, Exercise A

1. Didn't you work on Monday?
2. Don't you have to wear a uniform?
3. Haven't they opened the store yet?
4. Didn't he start his new job last week?
5. Hasn't she had a training session?

Page 42, Exercise B

1. Shouldn't
2. Didn't
3. Haven't
4. Can't
5. Hasn't
6. Aren't

Page 43, Exercise C

1. **A:** My new job isn't going very well.
   B: Why not? <u>Didn't you get the position you wanted?</u>
   A: Not exactly. I wanted to be a server, but I'm washing dishes instead.
   B: That's too bad. <u>Didn't you tell them you wanted to be a server?</u>
   A: Well, yes, but they need dishwashers right now.
2. **A:** I want to go to the party on Saturday, but I have to work.
   B: Oh no! <u>Didn't you tell your boss you needed that night off?</u>

   A: Yes, but I'm on the schedule.
   B: <u>Can't someone else work?</u>
   A: I don't know. I'm going to find out.

Page 43, Exercise D

Answers will vary, but could include:

1. Didn't your supervisor tell you how to do it?
2. Doesn't he usually finish by 7 P.M.? *or* Isn't he usually finished by 7 P.M.?
3. Didn't you tell your supervisor?
4. Don't they usually clean the kitchen at night?
5. Can't they hire more workers? *or* Shouldn't they hire more workers?
6. Can't you take a break?

Page 44, READ

☑ strains
☑ sprains
☐ burns
☑ repetitive motion injuries
☑ falls

Page 45, Exercise A

1. unsafe work practices, hazardous conditions, exposure to harmful chemicals
2. strains and sprains
3. clean wet areas immediately, be sure workers wear proper footwear
4. 7 to 8 hours of sleep a night

Page 45, Exercise B

1. . . . improper lifting and carrying heavy objects can cause serious injuries.
2. If you sit in a chair for long periods of time, make sure you stand up and stretch regularly.

Page 45, Exercise C

1. b
2. a
3. b
4. b
5. a

Page 46, Exercise A

Our manager asked the team **work / to work** faster. She **said / advised** us, "We aren't meeting our quotas. We all need to speed up." We asked her **suggest / to suggest** ways to work faster. We **said / told**, "We don't know how to work faster." She told us **help / to help** each other more. She **said / told** us, "If you help each other out, you'll work faster and meet your quotas." But, she also reminded us **not forget / not to forget** about safety. She **said / warned** us, "It's easy to forget about safety when you work quickly."

Page 46, Exercise B

1. asked us to summarize
2. told us to work
3. asked me to lead
4. said to write down
5. asked the group to discuss
6. advised everyone to review

Page 47, Exercise C

1. She told us to arrive on time.
2. She told us to wear comfortable clothes.
3. She asked us not to wear jeans.
4. She said to check the information sheet every day.
5. She instructed us to wash our hands before starting a shift.
6. She said to take a twenty-minute break every shift.
7. She asked us not to take a longer break.
8. She reminded us to sign our time card at the end of a shift.

Page 47, Exercise D

I was really nervous when I first started working as a server at Kip's restaurant. My boss, Terry, told me not **to** worry, but it was hard. Terry ~~ask~~ **asked** me to start by watching him take an order. He ~~said~~ **told** me to pay attention to how he wrote everything down. It seemed really easy when I watched him do it! Then, he asked **me** to take the next order. He advised me **to** repeat the order back to the customer to make sure it was correct. And, he reminded me not **to** be nervous. Of course, I was, but the customer was very nice and I didn't forget anything!

Page 48, Exercise A

Answers will vary, but could include:

Ways to make our office more environmentally friendly

Page 48, Exercise B

In our last meeting, we ~~discuss~~ **discussed** the problem of keeping the restaurant kitchen clean. Here ~~is~~ **are** some suggestions to solve this problem:

- Cooks shouldn't wait until the end of a shift to ~~cleaning~~ **clean**. We should ~~to~~ train new cooks to clean as they cook.
- We should schedule one cook to stay longer to clean at the end of each shift.
- We should assign one person to supervise and approve all cleaning.

Thank you for ~~consider~~ **considering** my suggestions. I hope we can discuss them next week.

Page 49, Exercise A

1.	f	3.	b	5.	a
2.	e	4.	d	6.	c

Page 49, Exercise B

1.	a	3.	b	5.	a
2.	a	4.	a	6.	b

Page 49, Exercise C

1. ask for clarification
2. meet / quotas
3. follow / instructions
4. solve problems
5. avoid delays
6. spend time

UNIT 5

Page 50, Exercise A

1.	g	3.	c	5.	e	7.	b
2.	f	4.	a	6.	d		

Page 50, Exercise B

1. You should know what to do if there is an emergency.
2. If you smell smoke, call the fire department.
3. If you hear the fire alarm, you need to evacuate the building.
4. Don't panic if you have to evacuate.
5. You might be in danger if you don't act quickly.

Page 51, Exercise C

Answers will vary, but could include:

1. If you have children, don't allow them in the kitchen when you are cooking.
2. If you see a fire, call the fire department.
3. If you hear a fire alarm, leave the building immediately.
4. If a pan catches fire, cover it and turn off the stove.
5. If the door is blocked, use the fire escape.
6. If there is smoke, get down low and crawl to the nearest exit.

Page 51, Exercise D

Answers will vary.

Page 52, READ

Answers will vary, but could include:

They prepared an emergency kit, so they were better prepared.

Page 53, Exercise A

b

Page 53, Exercise B

1. New Orleans
2. The first floor of their home flooded with water.
3. They listened to the news on the radio.
4. five days
5. Houston
6. stock up on food and water, own a battery-powered radio, prepare an emergency kit, create a disaster plan

Page 53, Exercise C

Answers will vary.

Page 53, Exercise D

1. seeping
2. utterly
3. reunited
4. stocked up
5. news bulletins

Page 54, Exercise A

Good evening, folks. Well, it looks like this wet weather will continue until we get to the weekend. But things will get better after this front has passed. It will be drier next week, but it'll be cooler, too, so you may want to take a warm jacket when you go to work on Monday.

We're also getting reports of some flooding in the northern parts of the state, so if you're heading up that way, check the forecast before you head out. We will let you know what's happening up there as soon as we have more information.

I'll be back with more weather after we've had the sports news, so stay tuned!

Page 54, Exercise B

I didn't know there was a tornado coming. I watched the news before / until I went to work, but I didn't hear anything about a tornado watch. But before / when I was at work, someone turned on the TV. I didn't pay a lot of attention as soon as / until I heard someone say, "There's a tornado in Somerville!" That's where I live. So

as soon as / before I heard that, I stopped working and watched the news report. It said that parts of the town had been damaged. I waited until / when the danger was over, and then I drove home. Until / When I got to my house, my wife was waiting for me. She was fine, and so was the house. So we went out to check on our neighbors. Before / When we saw what had happened to some people, we realized how lucky we were.

Page 55, Exercise C

1. When
2. Before
3. as soon as
4. until
5. After

Page 55, Exercise D

Answers will vary, but could include:

1. you leave your home
2. it's too late
3. go to a safe place
4. you may have to evacuate
5. emergency workers tell you it is safe
6. check to make sure everybody is OK

Page 55, Exercise E

Answers will vary.

Page 56, Exercise A

1. Seattle and New York
2. Partly cloudy
3. Minneapolis and Los Angeles
4. Miami
5. Los Angeles
6. Minneapolis
7. Sunny
8. Monday

Page 57, Exercise B

Answers will vary.

Page 57, STUDY SKILL

1. Honolulu
2. Minneapolis
3. Chicago
4. 6

5. partly cloudy
6. Houston
7. It will be cooler today and rainy.
8. warmer
9. no

Page 58, Exercise A

1. c
2. f
3. d
4. g
5. b
6. e
7. a

Page 58, Exercise B

1. Someone must be hurt. / It can't be serious.
2. It must hurt. / Could it be broken? / It might be sprained.
3. It might be. / Where could it be coming from? / It must be a fire.

Page 59, Exercise C

Answers will vary, but could include:

1. The cyclist must be hurt.
2. His leg might be broken.
3. The driver must be calling 911.
4. The woman must know the cyclist.
5. The older woman might be a doctor.
6. The mechanic must work in the auto repair shop.
7. The mechanic may have seen the accident.
8. The SUV might not be badly damaged.

Page 60, Exercise A

1, 3, 4, 2

Page 60, Exercise B

Is It is important to agree on a meeting place where everyone in your family can go in an emergency. That way, everyone knows where to go and family members do not have to travel around the city to look for each other. It's also a good idea to call an out-of-state friend or family member to let their them know you are OK. When there is an emergency, the telephone lines in your local area may not be working.

Page 61, Exercise A

1. h	3. g	5. a	7. e
2. c	4. b	6. d	8. f

Page 61, Exercise B

1. over
2. through
3. into
4. out of
5. past
6. under
7. off
8. away from
9. toward

UNIT 6

Page 62, Exercise A

1. Tenants are <u>required to pay the electricity bill</u> and to <u>pay a security deposit</u>.
2. Tenants are <u>not required to pay the garbage bill</u>.
3. Tenants are <u>permitted to have a bird or a fish</u> but they are <u>not permitted to have cats or dogs</u>.
4. Tenants are <u>required to give one month's notice</u> before moving out.

Page 62, Exercise B

1. Are we allowed to use
2. Each tenant is allowed *or* permitted to use
3. each tenant is allowed *or* permitted to use
4. you are allowed *or* permitted to park
5. Is he allowed *or* permitted to smoke
6. tenants are not allowed *or* permitted to smoke

Page 63, Exercise C

1. You're not allowed to use this door. You're supposed to use the other door.
2. You're supposed to put your trash in the trash cans. You're not allowed to leave trash on the floor.
3. You're only supposed to put paper in the recycling container. You're not allowed to put garbage in the container.
4. You're not allowed to park there. You're supposed to park on 10th street.

5. In case of emergency, you're not allowed to use the elevator. In case of emergency, you're supposed to use the stairs.
6. You're not allowed to smoke within 15 feet of the building. You're supposed to smoke more than 15 feet away from the building.

Page 64, Exercise A

- ☑ hanging laundry
- ☐ the cleaning deposit
- ☑ changing the locks on the doors
- ☐ the number of tenants in the apartment
- ☐ parking rules
- ☑ blocked water pipes
- ☑ noise
- ☐ lost keys

Page 64, Exercise B

1. No 2. No 3. No 4. Yes

Page 65, Exercise A

b

Page 65, Exercise B

1. noun
2. noun
3. verb
4. noun
5. verb
6. verb
7. noun
8. verb

Page 66, Exercise A

1. didn't you
2. did she
3. aren't they
4. is there
5. doesn't it
6. isn't he
7. did you
8. isn't there

Page 66, Exercise B

1. aren't
2. didn't
3. isn't
4. don't
5. did
6. didn't
7. was
8. do

Page 67, Exercise C

1. **A:** isn't it
   B: do you
   A: do you
2. **A:** do you
   B: aren't we
   B: won't you

3. **A:** don't you
   B: isn't it
   A: does it

Page 67, Exercise D

1. We have to fix the window, don't we?
2. James called the landlord, didn't he?
3. This apartment is cold, isn't it?
4. The neighbors aren't home, are they?
5. The neighborhood is a little noisy, isn't it?
6. The plumbers were here today, weren't they?
7. Lola sent in the rent check, didn't she?

Page 68, READ

Answers will vary, but could include:

Crime in the neighborhood forced residents to start a neighborhood watch group.

Page 69, Exercise A

- ☐ At Sunset Apartments, residents introduce themselves and bring food to new residents.
- ☐ Residents of Sunset Apartments got to know one another after starting a neighborhood watch group.
- ☑ Sunset Apartments is a special place because residents help one another and work out their problems.

Page 69, Exercise B

1. False
2. True
3. False
4. True
5. False
6. True
7. False

Page 69, Exercise C

1. e 2. c 3. d 4. a 5. b

Page 70, Exercise A

1. said
2. told
3. said
4. told
5. told
6. said
7. told

Page 70, Exercise B

1. Arthur said (that) the children are too noisy.
2. He said (that) his rent is too expensive.
3. He said (that) the teenage boy always takes his parking spot.
4. He said (that) his neighbor doesn't take out his trash.
5. He said (that) he doesn't like the carpeting in the hallway.
6. He said (that) his apartment always smells from his neighbors' cooking.
7. He said (that) the people downstairs always have parties on weekends.
8. He said (that) the building manager doesn't return his phone calls.

Page 71, Exercise C

1. was
2. were
3. asked
4. felt
5. would talk
6. was
7. knew
8. would talk

Page 71, Exercise D

1. Mrs. Yoon said that <u>someone was leaving the front door open</u>.
2. Ms. Price said that <u>she thought they needed to have another meeting next month</u>.
3. Mr. Kotov said that <u>people were parking right in front of the building doors</u>.
4. The building manager told the residents <u>she would post a notice about the parking problem and the doors</u>.

Page 72, Exercise A

Dear Ms. Chang:

I am writing to let you know that <u>the faucet in my bathroom sink is broken again. The handle doesn't turn off all the way and a lot of water is leaking</u>. I think it's getting worse.

<u>Could you please call a plumber to fix or replace the faucet? Or can we call a plumber and bill you?</u> The lease says that it is your responsibility. It needs to be fixed soon because we are losing a lot of water. Thank you. Please call me at (773) 555-1002. I look forward to hearing from you very soon.

Page 72, Exercise B

Dear Ms. Chang:

I **am** writing to let you know that my refrigerator is broken. It doesn't stay on all the time, so my food is going bad. I think it **is** getting worse. It ~~need~~ **needs** to be fixed or replaced. My lease ~~say~~ **says** that the landlord **is** responsible for making sure that all appliances work. Please call me at (773) 888-1000. Thank you. I look forward to hearing from you very soon.

Page 73, Exercise A

Answers will vary, but could include:

kitchen	living room
microwave	bookshelf
oven	coffee table
refrigerator	chair
chair	sofa
dishwasher	television
sink	fireplace

Page 73, Exercise B

	leaking	cracked	broken	burnt (out)	ripped
1. window		✓	✓		
2. bathtub	✓	✓			
3. carpet					✓
4. faucet	✓		✓		
5. microwave			✓		
6. sink	✓	✓			
7. lightbulb				✓	
8. curtains					✓
9. doorbell			✓		
10. toilet	✓	✓	✓		

UNIT 7

Page 74, Exercise A

1. buy
2. to drive
3. buy
4. to
5. than
6. to buy
7. to drive
8. look

Page 74, Exercise B

1. would you prefer
2. we'd rather
3. we'd prefer
4. would you rather
5. we'd rather not

Page 75, Exercise C

My wife and I are looking for a new car. There are a lot of options. I'd prefer **to** have a car that gets good gas mileage, even a hybrid if we can afford it. But my wife would prefer **to** have a big car that has a lot of space. She**'d** rather have a van, or an SUV, because they are more practical. Both of us are concerned about safety. We ~~had~~**'d** prefer to have air bags than air conditioning! And we agree that we**'d** rather buy from a dealer because a dealer would offer a warranty.

Page 75, Exercise D

Answers will vary, but could include:

1. I'd rather not have the compact car because it is too small.
2. I'd prefer the SUV because it has a lot of space.
3. I'd rather buy the SUV because there is a one-year dealer warranty.
4. I'd rather have a black car than a red car.
5. I'd prefer the SUV because it is safer. It has front and side airbags.

Page 76, LIFE SKILLS

Answers will vary.

Page 77, Exercise A

1. 56.8%
2. 18.3%
3. cars
4. cars
5. vans
6. less popular
7. SUVs

Page 77, Exercise B

Answers will vary.

Page 78, Exercise A

Mechanic: Greenville Auto Repair.
Liliana: Hi. I'm having a problem with my car and I think I'll have to bring it in.
Mechanic: All right, first tell me <u>what kind of problem you're having</u>.
Liliana: Well, my car is making a noise when I step on the brakes.
Mechanic: OK. Can you tell me <u>if it's been doing this for a long time</u>?
Liliana: I can't remember <u>when it started</u>. But I think it's getting worse.
Mechanic: Hmm . . . Do you remember <u>when you last had the brakes checked</u>?
Liliana: No, I don't. I just bought the car, so I don't know <u>what kind of work was done</u>.

Mechanic: It sounds like you need new brakes. Why don't you bring it in today? We'll take a look at it and tell you <u>how much it should cost</u>.

Page 78, Exercise B

1. I wonder what is causing the oil leak.
2. The mechanic can't figure out what the noise is.
3. Min-Ji is trying to find out if her car is ready.
4. Do you know how much a new radiator costs?
5. I don't remember when we bought it.
6. The mechanic is going to tell us whether the car needs new tires.
7. We don't know if we can afford a new car.
8. Cesar wants to know if we got a written estimate.

Page 79, Exercise C

1. if you can help me.
2. how many you want.
3. if I need to change all of the tires
4. what you think.
5. how much it will cost.
6. how long it will take.

Page 79, Exercise D

1. Omar is wondering what time he can pick up the truck.
2. Mary wants to know if her car is ready yet.
3. Patty is asking if he can change the oil, too.
4. Jin-Su is asking how much it will cost.

Page 80, READ

The author got the statistics from the National Highway and Transportation Safety Association (NHTSA).

Page 81, Exercise A

Circle the following:

inadequate surveillance 21%
distracted driving 14%
daydreaming 4%
driving too fast for road conditions 13%
misjudgment of others' actions or speed 89%
aggressive driving 2%

Page 81, Exercise B

1. drivers not paying attention to the road
2. distractions
3. Thirteen
4. tailgating
5. aggressive driving
6. distance monitors, lane monitors, blind spot sensors

Page 81, Exercise C

1. d
2. f
3. e
4. c
5. a
6. b

Page 82, Exercise A

1. The road <u>was</u> (2) slippery because it <u>had rained</u> (1) the night before.
2. The family <u>had</u> just <u>left</u> (1) home when the accident <u>happened</u> (2).
3. The driver <u>said</u> (2) that he <u>hadn't seen</u> (1) the cyclist.
4. Jackie <u>had heard</u> (1) about the accident on the radio, so she <u>decided</u> (2) to take a different route.
5. I <u>got</u> (2) a ticket because my registration <u>had expired</u> (1).
6. Carlo <u>ran out</u> (2) of gas. He <u>had forgotten</u> (1) to fill up the tank again!

Page 82, Exercise B

1. had been / had lost
2. had started / had checked / hadn't checked
3. had / stepped / had parked
4. had / had / had / gotten

Page 83, Exercise C

1. had just gotten
2. heard
3. looked
4. saw
5. had crashed
6. ran
7. explained
8. had run
9. wasn't
10. was
11. had never been
12. was
13. had only bought

Page 83, Exercise D

Answers will vary, but could include:

1. Olga had learned to drive before she came to the U.S.
2. The cyclist couldn't get up because he had hurt his leg.
3. Young Min didn't stop because he hadn't seen the sign.
4. Leanne had passed her driving test so she bought a car.
5. The traffic was backed up because there had been an accident.
6. After Eva had spoken to the police, they allowed her to leave.

Page 84, Exercise A

1. First
2. Then
3. then
4. After
5. Finally

Page 84, Exercise B

First, I spoke to my cousin, Dimitri. He is an auto mechanic, and he sometimes ~~have~~ **has** cars for sale. He told me that he can help me find a good car that ~~got~~ **gets** good mileage. After that, my family and I discussed how much ~~could we~~ **we could** pay. We didn't have enough money, so I ~~go~~ **went** to the bank to find out whether ~~could I~~ **I could** get a loan. I filled out some forms, and ~~get~~ **got** a loan for $5,000. Then my cousin and I started looking at used car ads on the Internet.

Page 85, Exercise A

1. sunroof
2. rear view mirror
3. windshield
4. windshield wipers
5. hood
6. side mirror
7. tire
8. fender
9. turn signal light
10. headlight
11. bumper
12. radiator

Page 85, Exercise B

1. *Headlight* is different because it's not a type of car.
2. *Tires* is different because the other words are all extras and not necessary.
3. *Hood* is different because the other words are safety items.
4. *Bumper* is different because the other words are insurance words.
5. *Brakes* is different because the other words are all liquids.
6. *Turn signal* is different because the other words are all paper documents.
7. *Estimate* is different because the other words describe a car.

UNIT 8

Page 86, Exercise A

1. How long have you been waiting?
2. Has she been feeling tired recently?
3. What have you been doing lately?
4. Has his leg been hurting only at night?
5. Have you been feeling any pain in your back?
6. What medication has Mrs. Lee been taking?

Page 86, Exercise B

1. hasn't been feeling
2. has been crying
3. has been holding
4. Has it been happening
5. Has she been sleeping
6. hasn't been waking

Page 87, Exercise C

1. Olga has been taking heart medication for two years.
2. I've been eating healthier food for a month *or* since last month.
3. We've been waiting at the doctor's office for an hour.
4. Tranh hasn't been feeling well since last night.
5. The children haven't been sleeping well for a few weeks.
6. My grandfather has been taking insulin since last year *or* for a year.

Page 87, Exercise D

Dear Juliana,

How are you? Have you been ~~feel~~ **feeling** better lately? I hope so! Things are fine here. Frank hasn't **been** working so hard, so that's good. Both of the kids have bad colds. Katie ~~haven't~~ **hasn't** been feeling well enough to go to school, but Leo has been ~~go~~ **going** to school. I've ~~be~~ **been** staying home from work with the kids, but I'll go back as soon as Katie is better.

How are you? What ~~you have~~ **have you** been doing? Write when you have a minute and let me know how things are going.

Xiao-Yan

Page 88, Exercise A

three

Page 89, Exercise B

1. True
2. True
3. True
4. False
5. False

Page 89, Exercise A

im•mu•nize /ˈɪmyəˌnaɪz/ v. [T] to protect someone from disease by giving him/her a Vaccine (SYN) inoculate, vaccinate: *Have you been immunized against tuberculosis?*

1.

med•i•cine /ˈmedəsən/ n. [CU] a substance used for treating illness: *Remember to take your medicine.* | *Medicines should be kept away from children.*

2.

in•oc•u•late /ɪˈnakyəˌleɪt/ v. [T] (formal) to protect someone against a disease by introducing a weak form of it into his/her body (SYN) immunize, vaccinate: *Children should be inoculated against measles.*

3.

vac•ci•nate /ˈvæksəˌneɪt/ v. [T] to protect someone from a disease by giving him/her a vaccine (SYN) immunize, inoculate: *Have you been vaccinated against measles?*

4.

Page 89, Exercise B

1. immunize, inoculate, vaccinate
2. medicine
3. immunize, inoculate, vaccinate
4. immunize, inoculate, vaccinate
5. medicine

Page 90, Exercise A

1. f
2. a
3. e
4. b
5. c
6. d

Page 90, Exercise B

1. such / so
2. so / so / so / such
3. so / such / so

Page 91, Exercise C

1. I'm so busy that I have to eat fast food.
2. I work such long hours that I don't have time to exercise.
3. It takes such a long time to get to the gym that I don't go.
4. Walking is so boring that I don't do it.
5. I'm so bad at cooking that I don't want to try it.
6. Fresh vegetables are so expensive that I can't afford to buy them.
7. I'm so tired after work that I just want to watch TV.

Page 91, Exercise D

Answers will vary, but ideas from the chart could include:

1. My doctor has such a busy office that it's hard to get an appointment.
2. I'm so tired that I don't want to go out tonight.
3. My sister is such a healthy person that she never eats fast food.

Page 92, READ

30 minutes a day or 30 minutes most days of the week

Page 93, Exercise A

1. about 45 minutes (of moderate activity) a day
2. Exercise helps people lose weight and stop smoking. It helps control high blood pressure and high cholesterol.
3. over 45
4. over 50
5. check with your doctor

Page 93, Exercise B

Answers will vary.

Page 93, Exercise C

1. c
2. d
3. e
4. a
5. b

Page 94, Exercise A

> **MEMO**
>
> To: All Parents
> From: Judith Chung, Principal
>
> Subject: Health and wellness for students
>
> We are implementing some new health and wellness strategies this year. Studies show that <u>students should be getting more exercise during the school day</u> and that exercise can actually help learning. Here are some new programs:
>
> - The gym will be open for an hour before school and an hour after school. Several teachers have volunteered to supervise. Students must wear athletic shoes or they will not be allowed into the gym.
> - We are offering exercise classes for the whole family on the first Saturday of every month. These are free, but <u>you should register in advance.</u> Classes fill up fast.
> - Good nutrition is a part of health, too. <u>We all should aim for at least five servings of fruit and vegetables daily.</u> The cafeteria will be offering healthful options to help with this. Please encourage your child to choose these healthful options.
>
> And, finally, a reminder that student health forms must be completed and handed in by September 8. Also, parents of new students must fill out a Family Data form by September 14.

Page 94, Exercise B

A. must / must
B. should
B. Should
A. should / had better

Page 95, Exercise C

1. You ought to *or* You'd better *or* You should get a flu shot.
2. You ought to *or* You'd better *or* You should go to the doctor.
3. You ought to *or* You should take a cooking class.
4. You ought to *or* You should go for walks together.
5. You ought to *or* You'd better *or* You should take some time off.

Page 95, Exercise D

Answers will vary, but could include:

1. They shouldn't sit in front of the TV for long periods of time.
2. They should play in the park together.
3. He'd better not eat so much junk food.
4. They ought to have a healthy meal together.
5. She shouldn't work so much.
6. She ought to leave work at five o'clock.

Page 96, Exercise A

Answers will vary, but could include:
Health care in Korea and the U.S.

Page 96, Exercise B

    The health care systems in Switzerland and the U.S. ~~is~~ **are** fairly similar. In both, you ~~buys~~ **buy** private insurance and there are different packages to choose from. And, in both countries, there ~~is~~ **are** a lot of problems because the cost is ~~such~~ **so** high. One big difference is that in the U.S. you often get insurance from your employer, but in Switzerland, you ~~doesn't~~ **don't**. Also, I was surprised to learn that there is dental insurance in the U.S. In Switzerland, we don't ~~has~~ **have** dental insurance. We have to pay for visits to the dentist.

Page 97, Exercise A

Answers will vary.

Page 97, Exercise B

1. tired
2. dizziness
3. Obesity
4. diabetic
5. sleepy
6. numb
7. weak
8. allergic

UNIT 9

Page 98, Exercise A

> **Greenville Elementary School**
> **Parents' Guide**
>
> Welcome to our school! As a parent, you are welcome on campus <u>because you are an important part of your child's education</u>. There are many things that you can do <u>to help your child succeed in school</u>. First, make sure that your child gets enough sleep, <u>since well-rested children perform better in school</u>. In the morning, make sure that your child has a good breakfast <u>so that he or she is ready to learn</u>. <u>Since children do not always tell you what is happening in school</u>, make sure you check homework, ask questions, and stay in touch with your child's teacher. Finally, read the school bulletins <u>to find out how you can volunteer at school</u>. Parents are an important part of the Greenville Team!

Page 98, Exercise B

1. c
2. f
3. b
4. d
5. e
6. a

Page 99, Exercise C

1. so that / because *or* since
2. so that / to
3. to / because *or* since / so that

Page 99, Exercise D

Answers will vary, but could include:

1. We wanted to speak to you because *or* since Alex is having some trouble in school.
2. We are meeting with Mi-Young's guidance counselor to discuss her college plans.
3. We'd like you to attend our Parents as Partners event so that you will learn our goals for the year.
4. My son gets into trouble at school because *or* since he is bored with his schoolwork.
5. Because *or* Since my son doesn't know anyone at his new school, we encouraged him to join some after-school clubs.

Page 100, Exercise A

four times per year

Page 101, Exercise B

1. fourth
2. counting whole numbers to 1,000,000
3. writing compositions and summaries of main ideas
4. multiplying and dividing two-digit numbers
5. extra tutoring
6. talk more

Page 101, STUDY SKILL

1. attending general meetings, attending scheduled meetings with teachers
2. acting as a volunteer or serving on a committee
3. 77%
4. 70%
5. increasing

Page 102, Exercise A

At our school, many parents participate in the school clean-up day. They vacuum (rugs) that have gotten dirty, repair (books) that have fallen apart, and do other (things) the teachers have requested. Some parents volunteer on other (projects) that benefit the school. For example, we have one (parent) who is a painter. He spent a weekend painting the school library using (paint) his boss had donated. Finally, the (school bake sale) is an event that everyone enjoys. It raises (money) the teachers need to pay for field trips.

Page 102, Exercise B

1. d
2. c
3. e
4. b
5. a

Page 103, Exercise C

1. that
2. that
3. reads
4. which
5. are
6. who
7. that

Page 103, Exercise D

1. We enrolled Sun-Young in a school that had good test scores.
2. Sue had a teacher who *or* that she liked.
3. The teachers meet in a room that *or* which is used for conferences.
4. Luis couldn't do the homework that *or* which the teacher had assigned.
5. There is a special program for the children that *or* who get good grades.
6. Carmen takes a bus that *or* which stops directly in front of her school.

Page 104, READ

1. The letter was written to persuade people to vote "yes" for the school budget.
2. The budget will keep class sizes low, pay for support staff, fund art, music and librarians, and increase teachers' salaries.

Page 105, Exercise A

Answers will vary, but could include:

1. teachers have more time to work with individual students
2. they help keep schools clean and safe
3. children who take art and music classes perform better in school
4. there is no art teacher and the librarian only comes one day a week
5. the cost of living is rising and teachers' pay has been at the same level for five years

Page 105, Exercise B

1. Fact
2. Fact
3. Fact
4. Opinion
5. Opinion

Page 105, Exercise C

1. c   2. b   3. a   4. d

Page 106, Exercise A

1. must have, must not have
2. shouldn't have, should have
3. might have, might not have

Page 106, Exercise B

1. shouldn't have
2. must have
3. should have
4. might have *or* could have / might have *or* could have
5. couldn't have

Page 107, Exercise C

Answers will vary, but could include:

1. The boys must have broken the window.
2. The children on the bus must have been throwing paper in the aisles.
3. The girl might have broken her leg.
4. The boys couldn't have gotten into trouble with the principal because they are smiling.
5. The boy must have fallen off the swing.
6. The man may not have known that school was closed.

Page 108, Exercise A

1. Exercise keeps teenagers healthy and physically fit. <u>1</u>
2. One possibility would be to hold fund-raisers, such as a bake sales or magazine drives. <u>2</u>
3. Success in sports helps children develop confidence and social skills. <u>1</u>
4. Another option is to ask parents to pay a small fee or to volunteer as a sports coach. <u>2</u>
5. In addition, studies show that teens who are involved in sports are less likely to use drugs. <u>1</u>
6. Finally, we could ask local businesses to donate money or sponsor a team. <u>2</u>

Page 108, Exercise B

We would like to encourage all parent<u>s</u> to attend our monthly PTA meetings. The PTA helps to raise funds for many program<u>s</u> and activities, and provide<u>s</u> money for classroom materials. The PTA also organize<u>s</u> volunteers to help at the Talent Show and other community event<u>s</u>. Most importantly, PTA meetings keep parent<u>s</u> informed about what's happening at school.

Page 109, Exercise A

1. enrollment
2. improvement
3. participation
4. supervision
5. assignment

Page 109, Exercise B

1. report card / grades
2. open house
3. conference
4. subject

UNIT 10

Page 110, Exercise A

My company recently implemented some new policies. The general manager <u>made</u> all supervisors <u>take</u> a workplace safety class. After we took the class, the general manager <u>had</u> us <u>review</u> safety practices with all our workers. Reviewing safety is always helpful, especially because it <u>gets</u> you <u>to discuss</u> why safety is important. One problem I'd had was that my workers often didn't wear all their safety equipment. However, after they were reminded why the equipment is important, it was easier to <u>get</u> them <u>to wear</u> it. I told them if we went one month with everyone wearing all safety equipment all the time, I would <u>let</u> everyone <u>take</u> an extra break for a week. We'll see what happens.

Page 110, Exercise B

1. let
2. had
3. had
4. got
5. had
6. made

Page 111, Exercise C

1. Jackie got the supplier to rush the order.
2. Jackie had Sufia and Bao help the new employees. *or* Jackie got Sufia and Bao to help the new employees.
3. Sufia made Carlos wear a uniform.
4. Sufia got Tony to work overtime on Saturday.
5. Bao let Ted and Jose take their lunch break. *or* Bao had Ted and Jose take their lunch break.
6. Bao let Mike leave work early.

Page 111, Exercise D

Answers will vary.

Page 112, READ

a man had a heart attack and a fire broke out

Page 113, Exercise A

Story 1
_3_ Hue collapsed.
_5_ Rodriguez performed CPR on Hue.
_4_ Rodriguez called 911.
_6_ Paramedics arrived.
_1_ Rodriguez became a supervisor.
_2_ Rodriguez learned how to do CPR.

Story 2
_4_ Gross activated the fire alarm.
_3_ Gross noticed the fire.
_5_ Gross closed the emergency doors.
_1_ A fire started.
_6_ Gross left the building.
_2_ The fire alarm failed.

Page 113, Exercise B

1. True
2. False
3. True
4. False
5. True
6. True

Page 113, Exercise C

1. e   2. a   3. d   4. c   5. b

Page 114, Exercise A

From: Doug Torres
To: All assembly line supervisors
Subject: Safety training for new employees

I would like to thank all of you for your hard work during our new employee orientation week. You should all be proud of yourselves. However, let us stop for a moment to remind ourselves of the importance of workplace safety. Many workers want to start working by themselves on the assembly line right away, but it's important that they have the right safety training first. We've had several new employees hurt themselves recently. I think we need to re-assess our training procedures to ensure that we're doing everything we can to prevent injuries. I've revised the procedures myself but I'd also like your input.

Page 114, Exercise B

1. himself
2. myself
3. ourselves
4. yourself
5. herself
6. yourselves
7. themselves

Page 115, Exercise C

1. her / herself
2. myself / him / him
3. them / themselves
4. yourself / yourself
5. himself / him

Page 115, Exercise D

4 P.M.—A young man with a bad burn came in. He burned ~~him~~ **himself** on chemicals at his job in a factory. Dr. Silvan told ~~himself~~ **him** that he needed to see a burn specialist.

5 P.M.—A father came in with his 9-year-old daughter who had a bad cut on her hand. The girl cut ~~her~~ **herself** when she was trying to help her mother make dinner. The girl needed 5 stitches and, for the first time, Dr. Silvan let me put them in by ~~my~~ **myself**! He said I did a good job, so I was proud of ~~me~~ **myself**.

Page 116, Exercise A

three

Page 117, Exercise B

1. Palace Restaurant
2. February 25, 2010
3. She was lifting a pot of boiling water.
4. no
5. two days

Page 117, STUDY SKILL

1. cooks, construction workers, nursing aids
2. construction workers
3. 10:01 A.M. to 12:00 noon
4. 4:01 A.M. to 6:00 A.M.
5. 3,000

Page 118, Exercise A

1. Could I talk to you this morning?
2. Why don't you take a break now?
3. Would you mind working on Saturday?
4. Why don't I finish this for you?
5. Would you mind closing the store tonight?

Page 118, Exercise B

1. Would you mind
2. Could
3. Could you
4. Why don't I
5. Why don't you
6. Could Salvador
7. Would you mind

Page 119, Exercise C

1. A: Could I borrow
   B: Why don't you look
2. A: Could you help
   B: Why don't you ask
   B: Why don't you wait
3. A: Would you mind showing
   B: Why don't you get

Page 119, Exercise D

Answers will vary, but could include:

1. Would you mind working my shift this Saturday?
2. Why don't I help you with your work?
3. Could I look at your employee manual?
4. Could you be sure to clean up the work area next time?
5. Why don't you go home early?

Page 120, Exercise A

first paragraph: P
second paragraph: C
third paragraph: S

Page 120, Exercise B

I've been **a** student at the school for a few months now. I'm worried about a safety issue that I've noticed. There ~~is~~ **are** only a few signs showing where exits are located and those are difficult to see. I think this ~~are~~ **is** dangerous. I ~~knows~~ **know** this is because the building is very old. There were probably more signs, but now they're gone or difficult to see. I think the school should ~~to~~ put up more signs, especially on the staircase. This would be easy and inexpensive and it would make the school a lot safer.

Page 121, Exercise A

1. *un-*	2. *im-*	3. *in-*	4. *il-*
unemployed unsafe unhealthy unsanitary	impolite impossible	incorrect inexpensive	illegal

Page 121, Exercise B

1. unemployed
2. illegal
3. impossible
4. unsafe
5. unhealthy
6. unsanitary
7. inexpensive

UNIT 11

Page 122, Exercise A

1. I was waiting for my friend outside my apartment when a police car stopped in front of the building. Three police officers went into the building where someone was having a party.
2. My father was taking the dog for a walk last night when he saw some teenagers. They were writing graffiti on a wall.
3. My son and his friend were riding the bus home from school when a fight started between two passengers. The fight was still going on when my son got off the bus.

Page 122, Exercise B

1. was going / asked
2. walked / were trying
3. was having / called
4. noticed / was shopping
5. were loitering / asked

Page 123, Exercise C

1. happened
2. was walking
3. heard
4. saw
5. was running
6. were chasing
7. saw
8. were running

Page 123, Exercise D

1. I was crossing the street when a police officer stopped me.
2. While we were waiting outside the store, we got a ticket for loitering.
3. Mrs. Jones was watching TV when she heard about the accident.
4. While Ali was sitting at a traffic light, a car hit him from behind.
5. Someone stole my purse when I was waiting at the bus stop.
6. Two thieves entered the store while Mr. Wong was working.

Page 124, Exercise A

stealing $50,000

Page 124, Exercise B

1. defendant, Dennis Johnson
2. defense attorney, Janine Smith
3. judge, Vera Samuels
4. witness, Francine Wu
5. prosecutor, Harry Garcia

Page 125, Exercise A

1. Norton was accused of murder.
2. of
3. There's very little crime in their neighborhood.
4. commit
5. prevention, rate
6. violent
7. The police have evidence that the killer was a woman.
8. of, for, against
9. have, give

Page 125, Exercise B

1. violent crimes
2. crime rate
3. committing
4. give
5. of, against

Page 126, Exercise A

When a citizen <u>is called</u> for jury duty, he or she must go to the court on a specific date. First, a prospective juror waits in a waiting room until his or her name <u>is called</u>. Then, the person <u>is sent</u> to the courtroom, where the prosecutor and the defense attorney <u>are introduced</u>, and where the prospective jurors <u>are given</u> some information about the trial. One by one, each individual <u>is questioned</u> to determine if he or she would be a suitable juror. If a juror has a good reason not to participate in the trial, he or she <u>is excused</u> and another name <u>is called</u>. This continues until all twelve juror seats <u>are filled</u>.

Page 126, Exercise B

STARSON APPEARS IN COURT

In a trial that **held /(was held)** today in Los Angeles, film star Lee Starson **accused /(was accused)** of shoplifting from a department store. Starson **(appeared)/ was appeared** in court wearing sweatpants and a T-shirt. Several witnesses **called /(were called)**. However, the case **dismissed /(was dismissed)**

LOCAL BUSINESSMAN ROBBED

Ron Delgado, owner of the Quik-bite restaurant chain, was the victim of a robbery last night at 11:15 A.M. Delgado **(was returning)/ was returned home** from work when he **approached /(was approached)** by two men who **(asked)/ was asked** him for money. When Mr. Delgado **(refused)/ was refused**, he **knocked /(was knocked)** to the ground and his wallet **took /(was taken)**. The men **(escaped)/ were escaped** in a gray van. Delgado **treated /(was treated)** for minor injuries at Greenville Hospital.

Page 127, Exercise C

1. were called
2. were arrested
3. was blocked
4. was called
5. were moved
6. was reported
7. was stopped
8. was charged
9. was found

Page 127, Exercise D

1. Fifty dollars was stolen from my wallet.
2. The suspects were arrested.
3. My car was damaged.
4. A trial was scheduled.
5. Several witnesses were called.
6. The defendant was brought in.
7. The evidence was heard.
8. The case was dismissed.

Page 128, READ

clients of the law office, people with questions about legal issues

Page 129, Exercise A

A defendant can be found guilty of perjury | if a jury can find that, | in the course of a trial, | he or she gave a knowingly false reply to a question; | in other words, | he or she lied on purpose | when the truth could have been told.

Page 129, Exercise B

1. misdemeanor
2. felony
3. attorney
4. perjury
5. judge
6. sentence

Page 129, Exercise C

1. c   2. e   3. b   4. a   5. d

Page 130, Exercise A

1. a   2. b   3. b   4. a

Page 130, Exercise B

1. as long as
2. even though
3. even if
4. As long as
5. as long as
6. Even though
7. as long as
8. even if

Page 131, Exercise C

1. even though
2. as long as
3. as long as
4. even if
5. even if
6. Even though

Page 131, Exercise D

Answers will vary, but could include:

1. the crosswalk is empty
2. there are no cars coming
3. it's not between 9:00 A.M. to 12 P.M. on a Monday
4. there is a parking space available

Page 132, Exercise A

Answers will vary, but could include:

The Legal Systems of the U.S. and Taiwan	
Taiwan	**The U.S.**
People can remain silent when questioned by police.	People can remain silent when questioned by police.
People can have a lawyer with them during questioning.	People can have a lawyer with them during questioning.
There is a judge in each courtroom.	There is a judge in each courtroom.
There is no jury; the judge decides cases.	A jury decides cases.
The judge, not the attorneys, questions the witnesses and defendant.	Defense attorneys and prosecutors question the witnesses and defendant.

Page 132, Exercise B

In Brazil, **the** first step in a legal process is a hearing, when the defendant goes before **a** judge who listens to the prosecution and the defense. The aim of the hearing is to decide whether or not a case needs to go to court. If the judge decides that a felony ~~have~~ **has** been committed, and that there is enough evidence to prosecute **the** defendant, he can set a date for a trial.

Page 133, Exercise A

1. e	4. a	6. b
2. f	5. c	7. d
3. g		

Page 133, Exercise B

1. dismissed
2. arrested / released / committed
3. pleaded / found / convicted
4. sued

UNIT 12

Page 134, Exercise A

1. an online account, a user name, a password, a representative
2. the enrollment form, the password
3. online banking, setting up, assistance
4. your account, our website

Page 134, Exercise B

A: I'd like some information about applying for **a** / the credit card.
B: Of course. Here's **a** / Ø brochure that describes a / **the** cards that we offer.
A: What is Ø / **the** interest rate on the rewards card?
B: Well, I can offer you **an** / Ø introductory rate of 1 percent. After three months, an / **the** interest rate will be between 10 and 20 percent, depending on your credit rating. I think you'll find that our **the** / **Ø** rates are very competitive.
A: OK, thanks. I'll take a look at a / **the** brochure and get back to you.

Page 135, Exercise C

Even if you usually pay with _Ø_ cash or use _Ø_ checks to buy things, it's _a_ good idea to build _a_ strong credit history. If you have good credit, it is easier to get _a_ loan for things like _a_ car, _a_ computer, or even _a_ new home. Also, _Ø_ employers may check your credit because _a_ good credit history shows that you are _a_ responsible person. _Ø_ Most landlords also check your credit because it tells them whether you will pay your _Ø_ rent on time. Credit cards let you buy items online and over _the_ phone, and you do not have to carry a lot of _Ø_ cash. And finally, credit cards are good to have in _Ø_ emergencies.

Page 135, Exercise D

Customer: I'm starting my own business. I'd like information about ~~a~~ business loans.
Loan Officer: Sure. Can you tell me a little about **the** business you're starting?
Customer: Well, it's **a** small grocery store.
Loan Officer: So you'll probably need to buy equipment like ~~the~~ **a** cash register and ~~the~~ **a** freezer. We offer **an** equipment loan that would be a good choice for you. You can pay back **the** loan in fixed monthly payments.
Customer: That sounds good. How do I apply for that?
Loan Officer: Here's a brochure about ~~a~~ **the** loans that we offer, and here is an application form. I'll help you fill out ~~a~~ **the** form if you like.

Page 135, Exercise E

Answers will vary.

Page 136, Read

Answers will vary, but could include: to help people choose a credit card wisely

Page 137, Exercise A

❑ Choosing a credit card is a difficult process, and companies will send you a lot of information to get you to choose their card.

☑ There are a lot of choices with credit cards. It's important to get information before you make your choice.

Page 137, Exercise B

1. a card with no annual fee and with a longer grace period
2. a card with a lower interest rate or APR
3. annual percentage rate
4. an annual fee, a cash advance fee, a balance-transfer fee, and a late payment fee
5. the number of days you have to pay your bill in full
6. rebates on purchases, frequent flier miles, and car rental insurance

Page 137, Exercise C

1. carry over
2. wisely
3. purchases
4. incentives
5. rebates

Page 138, Exercise A

1. e
2. c
3. d
4. f
5. a
6. b

Page 138, Exercise B

• **Make a budget.** Many people don't realize how important this is! If you don't / **won't** know how much money you need, you **don't** / won't be able to plan for saving.
• **Watch the little things.** It's easy to spend a lot of money on a lot of little things: coffee, snacks, etc. **You /** You'll be surprised at how much you can save if you don't / **won't** spend so much on little things.
• **A little adds up.** Our grandparents knew this but many of us have forgotten. If you / **you'll** save even a few pennies, **they /** they'll add up over time. Really, it's true!

Page 139, Exercise C

1. don't cut
2. won't save
3. sell
4. 'll have
5. get
6. 'll have
7. 'll have
8. have
9. cancel
10. 'll save

Page 139, Exercise D

Answers will vary, but could include:

1. He'll have less time to spend with his kids if he gets a second job.
2. If he sells his car, he won't have to pay for gas or insurance.
3. He'll have to wake up earlier and pay for bus fare if he sells his car,
4. If he doesn't visit his family in Mexico this year, he won't have to buy airplane tickets.
5. His family will be disappointed if he doesn't visit them in Mexico this year.

Page 140, Exercise A

$32,084

Page 140, Exercise B

Line 1: $32,084
Line 4: $32,084
Line 7: $6,372.54
Line 9: $6,372.54

Page 141, Exercise C

1. Clean Well
2. 33-0005555
3. $6,372.54
4. Box 4
5. $32,084
6. Line 9

Page 141, STUDY SKILL

1. housing and transportation
2. clothes and services
3. housing and food
4. clothes and services
5. health care, entertainment, food, housing

Page 142, Exercise A

1. e   2. c   3. b   4. d   5. a

Page 142, Exercise B

1. A: didn't have to / would have
   B: quit / wouldn't make / would be / didn't work
2. A: had / would take
   B: started / would have
3. A: had / would go / had / would look
   B: were / would be

Page 143, Exercise C

Answers will vary, but could include:

1. If In-Su had some extra money, he'd visit his family in Korea.
2. If Tatiana had more experience, she'd open her own café.
3. If Gail and Paul worked fewer hours, they'd spend more time with their grandchild.
4. If Safiya spoke better English, she'd take classes.

Page 143, Exercise D

Answers will vary.

Page 144, Exercise A

Circle: **Which organization would I choose if someone gave me $1,000 and told me to give it to charity?**
Circle: **I would give the money to Heifer International.**
Underlining will vary.

Page 144, Exercise B

If someone gave me $1,000 and told me to give the money away, ~~who I would~~ **who would I** give it to? I **would** give the money to my local homeless shelter. I think it ~~are~~ **is** important to focus charity on local problems because that is where individuals can make the most difference. My community ~~have~~ **has** a big problem with homelessness and there are several shelters that do good work. But the shelters never ~~has~~ **have** enough money, so I would ~~gave~~ **give** my money to one of these shelters.

Page 145, Exercise A

☐ 1. My friend Tia lent me her cell phone so I could call home.

☒ 2. I lent my computer from my friend Tia to do my homework.

☐ 3. I borrowed $20 from my friend Tia and I'm going to pay her back tomorrow.

Page 145, Exercise B

1. budget
2. overdraft
3. interest rate
4. cut down on
5. online banking
6. account balance
7. debit card
8. minimum balance